EASTERN SUN, WINTER MOON

Other books by Gary Paulsen

Gary Paulsen

EASTERN SUN,

A Harvest Book
Harcourt Brace & Company
San Diego   New York   London

WINTER MOON

AN AUTOBIOGRAPHICAL ODYSSEY

Requests for permission to make copies of any part of the work should be mailed to: Permissions Department, Harcourt Brace & Company, 6277 Sea Harbor Drive, Orlando, Florida 32887-6777.

Library of Congress Cataloging-in-Publication Data
Paulsen, Gary.
Eastern sun, winter moon: an autobiographical odyssey/by Gary Paulsen.—1st ed.
p.   cm.
ISBN 0-15-600203-5
1. Paulsen, Gary—Biography—Youth.   2. Paulsen, Gary—Journeys—Philippines.   3. Novelists, American—20th century—Biography.   4. Americans—Philippines—Social life and customs.   I. Title.
PS3566.A834Z464   1993
813'.54—dc20   91-47127

Designed by Lydia D'moch
Printed in the United States of America

First Harvest edition 1995
   B C D E

Foreword

It was in an old box in the basement of my sister's house in northern Minnesota, wrapped in plastic, mouse-chewed at the edges,
dusty gray and yellowing, fly-specked and dirty and tired and
brittle.

My life.

I thought that someday I would write of those first nine
years—the war and after—and that I might do it as an autobiog-
raphy, but there was still that hesitation; the wait right before
you jump off the edge of the mountain. A part of me wanted to
save it, to cloak it in small fictions, many small fictions, but my
sister called me one day. Mother had passed away, and then father, and she had been rummaging in a box.

"I've found all these old photographs from when you were
young. I thought you'd want them."

And there they were. I blew dust from the pictures, sat with
my sister and had tea, and looked at the bits of my world, my life,
and knew that I would write it then. Knew that I had to.

Mother had a box camera and I learned to use it when I was
six and took pictures that she had developed and left in cardboard

boxes, except for some she threw away, and it all came back in a flood, a surge of memory when I looked at the black-and-white images. The smells, the sound, the feeling, and *living* of it came back so that I could feel the thick jungle on my skin, taste the salty Pacific air on my tongue, hear my mother's voice and the even, straight tread of my father's footsteps on the board floor. I was, again, seven.

But still, still I hesitated and waited to write it. There were places too raw to pick at, I thought—wounds, scars, things to damage me—and I could hide them in fiction still or not speak of the rough parts and a friend said:

"No—you must tell it all. Every part of it."

Her name is Lenore Carroll and she is of course right, and I would like to dedicate the book to her; because without her saying that when she said it there would still be something held back and there would not be this book, which is written as openly and as honestly as I can write.

Thank you, Lenore.

EASTERN SUN, WINTER MOON

One

Mother and I spent the war years in Chicago. My father was on Patton's staff and left with him in 1939, just after I was born, to train and then to fight in Africa and Europe, and I did not see him to know him again until I was seven years old.

Mother worked at a munitions factory on swing shift, where she ran a machine that made belted twenty-millimeter ammunition, and an old woman named Clara would sit with me during the nights while she worked.

Clara did just that. Sat. She had hair out of her ears and nostrils and a big mole on her cheek and she did not read to me or cook for me or hold me or cuddle me. She sat. And drank red wine that she poured into a jelly jar from a big jug in a wicker holder she brought each night.

We would sit for hours listening to the radio, Clara staring off into space and drinking wine while I watched the illuminated dial as we listened to Jack Benny and Red Skelton. I would hold a tattered little stuffed dog that I called Dog that I could not be separated from, and when Clara wasn't looking I would sneak to the kitchen cupboard and get the box of Hi-Ho crackers and munch them quietly so she couldn't hear me over the sound of the radio.

I liked Red Skelton best, especially when he did Clem Cadiddlehopper, then Charlie McCarthy, and especially Mortimer Snerd. Clara made them funnier because she talked to all the programs, talked to all the characters while they were performing.

"Goddammit, Charlie," she'd say to Charlie McCarthy. "Don't you talk back to Edgar that way, you little wooden-headed son of a bitch . . ."

I don't know if she liked me or didn't like me—she never paid enough attention to me to know—but I know she only liked one character on radio. She loved Fibber on the "Fibber McGee and Molly" show.

"Jesus Christ, Fibber," she'd scream at the radio. "Don't let the bitch ride over you like that!"

I soon developed definite tastes and would mimic her as we listened to the shows, but she didn't hear me and I think now it must have been an odd picture: the two of us sitting in the half-darkened apartment, an old crone and a young boy, staring at the radio dial.

"Kick that wooden-headed son of a bitch in the ass, Edgar," Clara would yell.

"Asshole to Mortimer Snerd," I would yell—not understanding the mechanics of swearing.

Sometimes in the evenings when there were musical shows I would sleep. I liked some of the Andrew Sisters songs, and Jimmy Dorsey and Glenn Miller, but I had trouble staying awake through them, though sometimes Clara and I would sing along in a kind of unholy harmony, my childlike almost-soprano with her raspy wine throat.

Clara left promptly at midnight each night, wobbling on unsteady legs, and for a time I would be alone until Mother would come home about twelve-thirty. I was not lonely because I would sit on the couch and stare at the dial on the radio and the light kept me company. When Mother came she always brought me something—sometimes a candy bar or an empty shell casing from the factory—and she would sit and drink a cup of coffee while I ate the candy bar or examined the casing and she would tell me about what it was like to work in the factory.

"There are long lines," she'd say, "with hundreds and hundreds of people working on them, all making bullets. You've never seen anything like it."

At first when we went to Chicago and she worked she would stay home on the weekends when she didn't have to be at the factory. We were alone a lot then and she made me take naps in the afternoon with her, which I hated but she made me take anyway, and on one afternoon when I was supposed to be napping I found a part of Mother I had never seen but would never forget.

I had grown some wile, even that young, and had devised a way to sneak off. I would pretend to go to sleep, lying next to her in the bed, and when I did that she would doze off herself. These were warm summer afternoons in an unair-conditioned apartment, and the hot air off the street blew the cheap curtains in small puffs and dozing came very naturally for her after the hard work of the week. As soon as I sensed her going to sleep I would begin to slide toward the bottom of the bed, an inch at a time, until I made it to the foot of the bed and then carefully, so carefully, to the floor.

Freedom.

If I remained quiet she might sleep for an hour or more, and I could play and enjoy myself. I didn't often do anything wrong—played with toys on the kitchen floor where the pattern of the linoleum made lines that could become roads for my small metal cars and trucks and war toys—but sometimes other opportunities presented themselves.

On one afternoon I was successful and had begun to play

when I saw that the apartment door was open a bit. I decided to go outside. I grabbed my stuffed dog with one eye and dragged it bumping down the back stairs and out into the alley.

It was a wonderful, mysterious, and forbidden world—the alley. I was allowed to play outside only when supervised, or when Mother was awake, and now I seemed to be off on some great adventure. Near the apartment was a billboard with a large pack of Lucky Strikes in the green pack facing out to the street. The billboard angled back toward the apartment, and where it ran into the wall it made a hidden, darkened corner. I no sooner made the area next to the billboard when I had to pee, and I went back into the corner so nobody would see me.

I set Dog on the ground and was busy taking care of the problem when I sensed a dark shape looming in the opening between the billboard and wall and turned to see a man.

He was huge, and dark-ugly, and smelled of old wine and vomit and urine with dirt grimed into his face so hard it seemed to crack when he smiled. Yellow teeth. All ugly, and I had fear so that my feet seemed riveted to the ground.

"Well." His smile widened. "Fresh young meat . . ."

We were from a place where we did not understand such things as this man. Mother had once, quietly, simply, told me never to take candy bars from strangers but had never told me why—it seemed a very silly thing to tell me without a reason—but even with that ignorance I knew this man meant me harm and I grabbed Dog and tried to run past him.

It was no good. With one hand he clawed the back of my shirt and stopped me and lifted me off the ground, close to his face so I could smell the stink of him even more, and with his other hand he fumbled with his fly.

"It's perfect," he said. "Like Christmas, coming on you this way. Perfect."

And I should have run or kicked or screamed or done something, anything, but all I could do was hang there in fear, still holding Dog by one ear, hang like a mouse caught by a cat, waiting for something I couldn't understand to happen, stunned into shock, waiting, hanging and waiting, and something hit the man so hard in the back of the head that snot sprayed out of his nose.

"No!"

My mother's voice exploded in the small area, only it was more than her voice. There was some wild thing in it, some snarling ripping thing that made it powerful, all powerful, and when she hit the man again in the back of his head he dropped me.

"Run!" she yelled at me. "Run for the house!"

I took her at her word, but I only made the corner. There I stopped because a man and woman—the people who lived in the apartment across from us—were coming to help. I turned then, knowing I was protected, but if anybody needed help it was the man.

He was on the ground and Mother was kicking at him.

"Not with him, you son of a bitch," she screamed, "not with mine, you don't. Goddamn, goddamn, goddamn . . ."

And she kept kicking him even when he was down. Not just wild kicks, but careful ones. She walked around him, waiting until she could find an uncovered spot and then she would kick, hard and deep, in his groin, his back, and when he would move his hands to protect one area she would kick in another. And when at last his hands quit moving and he lay still she aimed careful kicks at his temples, aimed perfect, almost dainty kicks with the hard steel toe of her work shoes until he didn't move, didn't move at all, and I looked up to see her eyes then.

There was a great brilliant rawness in them, a wild anger and savagery that made my breath stop, and I felt sorry for the man without really knowing why. He could not win, could not live, could not be while she lived and she could get to him. The man could not *be*. It was not that she was killing him, though she was, and not that he was being punished for what he had done, or nearly done, to me—it was that he could not be, could not exist.

In her eyes, in her look, there was no room for him left in all the world. He would end.

"You bastard," she said in a low voice, almost a hiss, kicking him carefully. He had by this time messed his pants and the fresh smell of crap and piss filled the small space by the wall. "You son of a bitch, not him, not mine you don't, not ever you don't, not ever with mine you son of a bitch son of a bitch son of a bitch . . ."

And I think now he was dead, know now looking back that he was dead and gone. His head looked soft, pulpy, with spit coming out of his mouth, and the humanness was leaving him. But the couple who came to help took me away then so I couldn't see any more, took me back to our apartment.

A short time later Mother came back upstairs and sat with me in the kitchen chair next to the table with the oilcloth covered with blue leaves and cleaned her shoes with a damp rag from the sink, her fingers shaking.

"You must never do that again," she said when she was done, and I cried because of what I had seen, not in the old man and his death but in her eyes, cried because it frightened me, and she held me while I cried it out. I was more afraid now than I had been while it was happening.

"What was that man going to do to me?"

But she didn't answer. She held me close and rocked back and forth while I cried. And then she made some Ovaltine and I drank it while she went out in the hall to talk to some police who came to the door.

When the police were gone she came back and we sat at the table and drank more Ovaltine and she told me about working at the factory. I know that she was talking to make me forget the man in back of the billboard, but it didn't work.

I would never forget him, would never forget the stubble on his face and the smell of him, the urine-whiskey stink of him while he held me up; and that night when I was in the small bed in the back of the bedroom I lay awake for a long time holding Dog and could not sleep.

After a time Mother came in from the kitchen and took me in her arms and held me on the big bed until finally my eyes closed and the pictures faded.

Two

We lived all of the hot summer in Chicago. There was steamy humidity whenever I went outside to play army. I had a fiber helmet liner that wobbled on my head and a wooden rifle with a brass-painted bullet that went back and forth when I worked the bolt, and I killed many enemy soldiers the first part of that summer.

It was 1944 and the soldiers invaded Normandy and I knew that Father was there. We had a picture of him on a shelf over a window so I knew what he looked like and I thought of him invading Normandy.

I did not know what a Normandy was, or how it should be invaded until Mother took me to a Roy Rogers movie and I saw a newsreel showing men running out of boats onto a gray beach and Mother cried and told me that was Normandy.

After that I imagined my father going onto the gray beach, running out of the boat, and I pretended to be with him and invaded Normandy again and again the first part of that summer.

Father wrote perhaps three times and Mother read me the letters, but on the third letter there was a change. She read most of it then skipped a large part and began to cry, sniffling, before she began to read again. But now the words came flat and I could see that the letter bothered her but didn't know why, and not long after that she began to change.

She seemed to spend more hours at work and would come in later, after I was asleep, and I could smell beer on her breath. She had never had beer on her breath before and it had a flat grain smell to it that I didn't enjoy—like stale breakfast food or sour breath from milk burps.

She would come in late and fumble around in the kitchen part of the room and wake me, except I didn't get out of bed and pretended to be still asleep. Then she would make coffee and always seemed to let it boil over and swear to herself, and when the coffee was done and the smell filled the whole apartment she would come into the small darkened bedroom and stand over me.

She breathed through her mouth, I think because she was trying to be quiet so she wouldn't wake me up, but I was always awake and heard her rasping breath.

After she stood over me for a time that seemed very long, she would come to the bed and lean across me and tuck Dog in closer to my side. And even with the drinking and being late and not telling me about working at the factory anymore it wasn't too bad because of that tucking in, her hands on the blanket and the smell of her pushing the silky little edge under my chin and around Dog.

On the weekends we no longer stayed in the apartment. During the days when it was warm we sat for the afternoon on the back steps and listened to the sound that came from the street. Mother would make me toast on a toaster that sat on the burner of the stove with four sides that tipped in and put peanut butter and grape jelly on it and give me a glass of milk. We'd sit on the back steps and I would drink the milk and eat the toast and listen to the Italian women yelling at their children and each other.

Sometimes when their voices mixed just right you couldn't

hear words but it sounded like music; all the words rose and fell together and I sat one afternoon and started humming and singing with the way the music sounded to me.

"What's that?" Mother asked. She was sipping a beer she'd bought at the store under the counter. I had asked her, when she told me about the grocer selling beer under the counter, why he did that but she didn't answer. "What's that song?"

"It's them," I answered, pointing at the street and all the people yelling at each other. "It goes back and forth and up and down and makes me want to sing."

"Why, that's pretty, like something you'd hear on the radio. Sing some more for me."

And so I did and that's how we started singing for dinners even though Mother didn't call it that. There were many songs that I had learned listening to the radio with Clara, and on weekend nights Mother would take me to a tavern on the corner, called the Cozy Corner. I had a small army uniform and she would dress me in it, take me to the bar, and put me up on a barstool and tell me to sing.

I would start with the song about mares eating oats and goats eating oats and then sing "Itty Bitty Fishes" and men would come to watch us. Many of them looked at Mother more than me, but they would put money on the bar and even though Mother was working and didn't need the money she never turned it down. When there was a pile of quarters and sometimes even a dollar or two on the bar we would stop and Mother would order me a plate of southern fried chicken and french fries and a Coca-Cola in a bottle.

If we could have left right after the chicken and singing that would have been fun. The chicken had a crisp batter that was crunchy and kept the meat hot and steamy, and the french fries were hot and greasy so they held lots of salt, and the cold Coca-Cola seemed to make it all taste even better, but we didn't leave. We didn't leave.

After I stood on the barstool and sang and we ate, Mother would go to a booth and the men would come and sit with her and tease me about being in the army because I was wearing a uniform. When I told one of the men that my father was in the army and that I wanted to be like him even though I had never met him, the man got a strange look in his eyes and stared out the window of the bar into the street outside, and when I asked another man why he wasn't in the army—I thought everybody would want to be in the army fighting the krauts and nips—he told me his job was too important and that he had a bad back and that his feet were flat. Later I asked Mother how he could work if he had all those things wrong with him and she said he was fine and that he was just feeling guilty about letting other men like Father fight for him. I understood that, but when I asked Mother about all the other men that came to the booth and wanted to talk to her, asked if they were all guilty, she told me to hush and eat my chicken.

Then there came a time when nothing worked right. Mother hadn't heard from Father and she had to work overtime so we didn't get to go to the Cozy Corner to get fried chicken and the radio broke and we couldn't listen to our shows and Clara got mad, and one night I awakened to hear Mother crying out in the other room.

I grabbed Dog and went to the door and peeked out and she was sitting alone at the table. In front of her was the picture of Father and there was a letter lying on the table and she had tears on her cheeks. I walked out of the room and up to her, and I knew she felt bad because she didn't even tell me to go back to bed.

Instead she held out her arms and took me into her lap. She pulled me in close and cried and cried and when I asked her why she was so sad her words came close and mixed with the crying.

"It's just the war, the damn war, and I'm so lonely, Punkin, so damn lonely, and Daddy has another . . . friend . . . in France."

It all didn't make much sense to me then. I couldn't figure

what was wrong with Father having another friend while he fought Germans in France and I said so, but Mother just held me and cried until I couldn't keep my eyes open and I went to sleep cuddled in her lap, holding Dog tight and thinking of Father and his new friend.

That weekend Mother didn't have to work overtime, and on Saturday night we went to the Cozy Corner. I stood on the stool and sang along as the pretty lights swirled on the jukebox and then had some fried chicken and french fries.

Mother drank beer and more beer. We moved to a booth and the man who owned the tavern brought tall dark bottles of beer and a Coca-Cola in a bottle for me and other men came to sit with Mother. I didn't like them because they sat closer and closer and tried to touch her more and more and they were rough men. There were hard movements of their hands when they pushed around me to get close to her and in their eyes when they said hello to me and they didn't drink as much as Mother and their necks seemed to get thicker and I liked them less.

Mother started to dance with them. At first it was all right because the music was fast. They did the lindy and some jitter-bugging and Mother would fly around the floor with her skirt out in a big circle so you could see her panties and her long blonde hair swirled out to the sides and she was beautiful. Even I could see it. She looked like pictures of movie stars in *Life* magazine where they held cigarettes and said they were waiting at home for their man. There was a red flush in her cheeks and her blue eyes were wide and happy and she moved so fine the music seemed to come from her, inside of her.

But then the music slowed down and the men started to take turns dancing closer with her, close and tight, and one man took her in his arms and the other men moved off because he was big and his arms seemed to almost wrap around Mother.

He was tall, so tall he had to stoop over and down to Mother, and he had big hands that held her in close and seemed to control her. His hair was short on the sides but long on top and so blond it was almost white. It was combed back on the sides in soft waves but part of it had fallen and he kept tossing back a piece of hair that hung over his eyes. He had blue eyes, a little red around the sides, and large teeth that showed wide when he smiled.

His name was Casey.

Mother kind of folded into him in a soft way, and her eyes turned all fuzzy when she looked up at his face and I knew about that look. I had seen it in movie posters when Mother took me walking downtown one Sunday afternoon and we went to a movie; seen the look in the movie posters when the woman was looking up at the man holding her.

When the music was done Casey put another nickel in and played another slow song and I sat and drank Coca-Cola and watched them dance and wanted the night to end. But it didn't.

They danced and danced all night, bringing me Coca-Cola and Oh Henry! candy bars until I was sick with them, and Mother didn't look at me once. Finally I went to sleep in the corner of the booth and didn't wake up until Casey was carrying me out of the bar late at night and up to our apartment. Mother put me in my bed in the bedroom and tucked me in tight with Dog and then went out into the other room with Casey, but I didn't sleep. I couldn't sleep.

I had slept hard in the bar and even when I closed my eyes and tried to think of nice things and slow things, which Mother made me do sometimes when we took naps and I couldn't sleep, it still wouldn't come. I lay awake in the room with the blue light from the sign out in front for the laundry down below blinking on and off, making the room go blue and then red, and I couldn't sleep. And then the sounds came.

From the other room. They were strange sounds that I hadn't heard before and Mother was making them. Moaning sounds. I held my breath and listened to the sounds. They started low in a kind of choking moan but grew, and I thought she was in pain. I climbed out of bed and took Dog by the leg and went to the door and opened it slowly to look out.

Casey was looking right into my face.

Mother was on her back on the old sofa with all her clothes off and the top of her head in my direction so she couldn't see me. She had her legs spread so one leg was on the floor and the other was up and over the back of the couch and Casey was between her legs. He had his clothes off as well and he was pushing down into her, holding himself up on his hands and arms and thrusting down and up and down, and when I opened the door he looked right at me, right into my face.

And he smiled.

I stood and watched and he kept moving up and down between my mother's legs, kept looking at me and smiling and thrusting until his eyes suddenly seemed to go out of focus and he grunted and thrashed up and down harder and then fell on top of her and all the time of it, all the forever and ever long time of it, I stood and watched him and he looked at my face and smiled and I couldn't say, couldn't do anything. Couldn't move.

When he was still I stood for a few more seconds and then turned and went back into the room and closed the door and climbed into bed and was mad and hated Casey and hated Mother. I did not understand what I had seen then, but it made me hate Casey and hate Mother and I wished that the krauts or nips would come and kill Casey and maybe spank Mother so she wouldn't lie on the couch on her back anymore and let Casey between her legs.

Three

"I have wonderful news," Mother said to me a week after I had seen her and Casey on the couch. "Casey is coming to live with us."

I didn't say anything but wished he would die. He stood next to Mother while she told me he was coming to live with us and smiled and smiled at me. I thought, *Sure, you son of a bitch big-tooth bastard asshole fucker fart, sure you can smile at me, but I hate you and I hope the krauts or nips come or maybe my father comes and kills you.*

But I said nothing, even when Mother told me later I must be nice to Casey and call him Uncle Casey because she liked Casey very much and he helped her to not be lonely.

And I guess Casey tried to be nice to me. He brought me all kinds of candy and Coca-Cola and taught me how to pour Planters peanuts in Coca-Cola and drink and eat the peanuts at the same time. He took us to Abbott and Costello movies and Roy Rogers movies and laughed and tickled me and bought me Hershey bars and popcorn and Oh Henry! candy bars until I thought I would puke but I still hated him.

He lived with us for all of that winter while Mother worked at the munitions plant. Casey moved into the bedroom with Mother and I slept on the couch and listened each night to Mother making the moaning sounds while Casey got between her legs, and I wished they would both die but they didn't.

One night while Mother was working I was listening to the radio with Clara. It was a whole program of songs about missing soldiers and I started to cry thinking of Father and Mother and Casey and how nobody was missing Father. I crawled into Clara's lap with Dog, crying and listening to the radio, but Clara seemed not to notice me and went along drinking red wine over my head and humming with the music.

I don't know how long it could have lasted but there came a day when all the people in the street came out of their apartment buildings screaming and laughing and crying and dancing, and Mother told me the war was over in Europe and the Germans had surrendered and Father would be coming home soon.

We were in the kitchen when she told me and Casey was standing next to her and it looked like a knife had gone into his stomach when she said it. His eyes tightened at the corners and he said:

"Shit . . ."

Mother looked at him and she started to cry and they hugged each other. Then Mother picked me up and hugged me as well, while Casey stood next to us like he didn't belong. And he must have felt the same thing because he turned away and went into the bedroom. Mother and I sat in the kitchen—she was holding me tight—for two or three minutes and Casey came out. He had a suitcase.

"If I forgot anything I can get it from you later," he said. He looked at Mother for a long time and the corners of his eyes were sad and down and for a moment I felt bad for him. Then I remembered the sounds from the room and Mother's legs when I saw them on the couch and didn't feel sad any longer.

He left without speaking, but Mother held me and cried for a long time after he left and I don't think she was crying because the war was over and Father was coming home so much as because Casey had gone, but I didn't care. Casey was gone and I didn't have to hear the sounds anymore.

Casey was gone and the war was over and Father was coming home and I didn't care about anything else.

Four

Letters came like snow for the next two weeks. It seemed like each day when Mother went down to the mailbox there would be two, three, and sometimes even four letters from Father.

We would sit at the kitchen table to read them. Mother made me Ovaltine and she made herself a cup of coffee. Then she would arrange the letters by the dates on the envelopes and read them to me, each and every one, and only leave out small parts here and there that she said Father only wanted her to hear.

They were wonderful letters. He wrote about the war only a little, but there was a lot about the country he was in. He said there were orchards and grapes all over and he was staying for a time in a place that had been almost a castle. I had pictures of knights in armor and dragons that Mother had shown me in a magazine one time, but she said it was more like a movie we'd seen with Casey all about a woman who lived in a villa in France.

He wrote about General Patton. Father was on Patton's staff—which she said had something to do with planning. He'd been promoted from a sergeant to an officer—which made me very proud—and then transferred from his unit up to work on the staff. It was all confusing to me, but I had seen pictures of General Patton in *Life* magazine so I knew what he was like: all military and with a steel helmet on and pearl-handled pistols and holding a pair of binoculars in front of his eyes. He always looked very dashing, but Father said in one of his letters to Mother that he was a huge pain in the ass. Mother read me that part without thinking, but she wouldn't let me repeat it, though I knew how to say ass and lots of other swear words from sitting in the Cozy Corner while Mother drank with the men from the factory who had swollen necks and looked at her funny. I didn't say them except when I was alone or with Clara, who didn't hear anything I said anyway, and then I would practice.

Father said he had lots of close friends killed in the war and that he was glad it was over and that he was looking forward to seeing us very much and finally, at the bottom of a letter, he said he wasn't coming home.

He stuck it on that way. I had lots of friends killed in the war, he wrote, and I'm not coming home. When Mother read that her voice kind of stopped and she looked at the door and I wondered if she was thinking of Casey.

Then she went on.

Father had been reassigned to the Philippine Islands to help with the rebuilding of the government in some way and he had to fly right across and wouldn't even have time to stop and see us. I thought it meant he would be working on some big government building—like the Chicago Museum where Mother had taken me once—and I was proud because I didn't know he knew how to rebuild buildings. But I was wrong. Mother said it was to work with people more than buildings and then she got to the bottom of the letter and let out a funny sound.

"Listen to this," she said, reading. " 'You and the boy will be getting travel vouchers in a day or two and you will proceed to San Francisco where you will find a ship waiting to take you to the Philippines. There is a long waiting list for seats on any planes for dependents and a ship is all we could get. Bring what you think you'll need for two years. I'll see you both in Manila.' " She took a deep breath and her eyes were shining. "Oh, Punkin, we're going to the Philippines to be with Daddy. Isn't that wonderful?"

Of course I thought it was wonderful to be going to see Father, even though I didn't know what a *manila* was—unless it was some kind of ice cream—and I had only one question.

"Can I bring Dog?"

Five

There were crowds everywhere, huge jams of people in cities and train depots waiting to come home from the war or to get to places where they could meet people coming home from the war. When we came to the depot in Chicago with our boxes and suitcases I had to hang on to Mother's slacks to keep from getting lost in the crowds. Hundreds of men in uniform ran or sat or slept in the depot, and a good many of them whistled at Mother.

Mother could not find a seat on a train all the way west. We made our way as far as the train depot in Minneapolis—where we arrived at midnight—but all the trains west to San Francisco were filled and would be filled for days, even those without sleeping berths where we would have to just sit in seats the whole way. We slept for one night in the depot along with men in uniform, packed in rows of benches. I looked for Father, thinking he might come through this way—not understanding that he was already in the Philippines—but I had never seen him to remember him and had only the small picture Mother had kept on the table by the window with the flag and star for reference.

And there were so many men. Sailors and soldiers and marines, hundreds and hundreds, all waiting for trains and all very, very nice to me and even more nice to Mother.

"We have to get to San Francisco in a week, Punkin," she said, "or we'll miss the ship and then I don't know what we'll do . . ."

I did not know where San Francisco was but could tell from her voice that she was terribly worried and wished I could help her, but all I could do was sit by the suitcase holding Dog and look at the high ceiling of the depot and all the uniforms of the waiting men.

She checked with the ticket agent often to see if there had been any change, standing in line while I waited with the suitcase, and when she came back from one of the attempts, shaking her head and near tears, a soldier in a brown wool uniform came up to her.

"Ma'am, my name is Matt. I couldn't help overhearing that you are having some trouble getting to San Francisco."

Mother nodded. "Yes. All the trains are full and the military has priority."

He shook his head. "Not all of us. I'm trying to get out there and so are two or three other guys, and they won't even talk to us. The thing is, I wanted to buy a car anyway with my mustering-out pay. So I thought if I bought one some of you could chip in and help with the drive out. Would you and the boy like to go with us?"

"All the way to California?" Mother said. "It must be two thousand miles."

Matt nodded. "But if we keep driving we can probably beat the train . . ."

Mother hesitated—two beats, perhaps three—then nodded. "We'll go."

There were no new cars. They had stopped making new ones when the war started, so all cars were at least five years old, which made driving across country on the narrow, cracked high-ways a major trip.

Only one other man finally went with us. He had one hand gone—which I thought was fascinating and wanted to know about but which got me thumped, hard, on the head by Mother when I asked. It was still in a bandage and a sling but I could see where it ended, just ended, at the wrist, and try as I might I couldn't keep from looking at it. His name was Carl and I don't think he said ten words the entire trip. He kept taking pills, little white pills and large white pills and small yellow ones. Every time he awakened to where he might be on the edge of talking he'd take a pill and go back to sleep.

The car was a 1940 Ford sedan, black, with a pointed grille. Matt went to buy it while we waited at the depot. And when he came back for us Mother sat in front with Matt so she could change off driving with him and I sat in the rear with Carl, looking at his arm. They piled suitcases and duffel bags in the small trunk and around me so that I just about couldn't move and we started off.

There were two flat tires but aside from that the car worked perfectly the entire way—the long, long, impossibly long way for a six-year-old boy slotted into the backseat.

I had to pee right away, of course, and then had to pee again and again and finally they found me an old lard can and when I had to pee I would use the lard can and then throw it out of the window, hoping that the spray wouldn't come back into the car and hit me in the face, which it did if the wind was wrong.

Flat. For a long time, for all of the time in the world, it was flat. The Ford ground along, the engine whining out across the country through a day and a night and another day.

Sometime in that first night Matt pulled over to the side of the road and I awakened to see him lean toward Mother and turn her head and kiss her, and I thought of Uncle Casey and wondered if this would be that way, but it wasn't. She pushed him away and shook her head and hit him somewhere in the side below the seat where I could not see, and Matt nodded and smiled and turned back.

"Can't blame a man for trying."

"Yes," she said. "I can. This is a ride out West, no more."

"You've got it." He turned to the wheel and continued driving and I leaned against Carl and went back to sleep and did not know anything again until I opened my eyes to find daylight and more flatness and Mother driving.

She lighted a cigarette with a Zippo lighter, turning her head to get out of the wind and the flame that blew sideways, and saw that I was awake.

"Morning, Punkin." She used a long nail to pick a piece of tobacco off her lower lip, flicking it out the window as she turned back to driving. Her hair, long and blonde, blew around her face in the wind and she shook her head to make it move away and I thought she looked just like a movie star. "How are you doing?"

"Fine. I have to pee, though."

"Use the can. We have to keep driving while it's cool in the morning. Matt"—she pointed next to her where Matt leaned against the door asleep—"says we may have to stop for a while this afternoon when it gets hot and we're in the mountains because the car might heat up in the climbing."

"I saw him kiss you." I didn't know why I said it. I hadn't planned to, but it slipped out.

"You did, did you?"

"Yes. And then I saw you hit him."

"He didn't mean anything by it."

"I don't like it when that happens. It makes me think of Uncle Casey."

"That's all done, Punkin. All of it."

"I'm glad."

"So am I . . ."

By the middle of the afternoon we came to the mountains. When they were still a blue line in the distance it became so hot that even the wind whistling through the open windows felt like fire. We stopped at a gas station and café in the middle of nowhere, where they had a dog Mother wouldn't let me pet, and ate some greasy meat and potatoes with thick gravy that I threw up later out the back window, and Matt added water to the radiator of the car. In the café a cowboy wearing a cowboy hat made eyes at Mother and drew a picture of a bucking horse on a piece of a paper sack for me that was so real you could see the dust under the horse's hooves. But Mother just ignored him and he went away.

By the end of the third day we had passed through the mountains. When we came to the top it was cool and you could see the whole world and there was snow on the peaks though it was summer.

"See the snow, Punkin?" Mother asked. "Doesn't it look pretty? It's so bright and clear—sometimes it's hard to believe there ever was a war."

"There was, believe it." Matt stretched in the seat. "There really was a war. A big goddamn war, and all the pretty mountains in the world won't change it." His voice was flat, dead sounding, and Mother glanced at him and then back out the windshield and said no more about the war. I looked at Carl and thought he might say something about war because of his wound, but he was asleep.

We spent the rest of that afternoon winding on the narrow roads in the mountains and I became sick, puking out the back window again and again. Mother thought it was carsick, like it was when I threw up the greasy meat and potatoes, but I knew it was different because I felt hot and weak, so when we were in the desert Mother had me stripped to my shorts and eating aspirin to make me cool down. That's when she found the spots.

They went across my chest and stomach and up my neck and because it was so hot they seemed to spread fast.

"What is it?" Matt asked.

"I think it's chicken pox," Mother answered. "Do they itch bad, Punkin?"

I shook my head. "No. But I feel awful and it's so hot."

"It will cool soon, Punkin. We have to keep going."

We arrived in San Francisco two days before the ship was to sail and Mother found a room in a cheap hotel where all the people spoke Chinese and an old Chinese woman brought something hot in a bowl to the room not two hours after we arrived.

"For boy," she said. She had skin like wrinkled leather and eyes that lifted at the corners and looked like she had been laughing all her life. I was standing by the door and I reached for the bowl, but Mother pushed her away, smiling.

"For boy, for boy."

And finally—I think to smooth the situation more than anything—Mother relented. After first tasting the liquid herself, she handed me the bowl. "Just a sip, Punkin."

It tasted salty but good, and I drank most of it and in a short time seemed to feel better although I think much of it had to do with the old woman's eyes. They made me want to smile.

"We have to go to the Presidio and see about the papers and get ready to go. Tomorrow we get to ride the cable cars—won't that be fun?"

Early the next morning we went to the Presidio where the army had some brass cannons and a fort. There we were shuffled from building to building while Mother filled out form after form while I sat in big gray chairs and looked at all the soldiers in uniform. Finally we came to a long, low building with a red cross on the door.

"The doctors want to look at us," Mother said. "And give us some shots."

"Shots?" I held back.

"Yes. We have to have shots to ride on the ship."

"Shots?"

"It will be fine . . ."

"Shots?"

She dragged me into the dispensary where a nurse helped her to take my jacket and shirt off so the doctor could examine me.

He was a tall, thin man, with a face that made it look like he was going to cry. He shook his head slowly after he examined my chest, the spots, and listened to me with his stethoscope.

"I see we've got chicken pox."

I started to say that I didn't know he had them too, that I'd caught them in a car when I was puking all the time and where did he get his, but something in Mother's eyes made me keep my mouth shut.

"That makes for a problem," he said.

"He's on the way up now," Mother said. "The fever is gone and he seems better."

"I agree. In a week or so he'll be back to normal, if you keep him quiet. But there's a rule about diseases."

"What rule?"

"You're not supposed to allow anybody with a communicable disease to leave the country." His voice was flat and he looked out a window. "It's the law."

"Does that mean we can't go?"

"The law says not until the marks are gone."

"But that will be after the ship sails." Mother's voice was rising and I wondered if we didn't go if that meant we didn't have to take the shots. I didn't want to think about the shots, but they kept coming into my mind and I looked for the nurse with the needle, who I was sure was hiding around a corner.

"We'll miss our ship and God knows when we'll get another one . . ."

The doctor nodded. He had a reflector attached to a band on his head and it caught the light and flashed it on the wall and made a round dot that moved up and down. I watched the spot.

"That's why I'm going to leave the place where it says

'diseases' blank," the doctor said, his voice still flat and even. "It's the law. If I put anything down the law will take over."

At first Mother didn't say anything, but I saw her eyes become wet. "Thank you."

"Isn't chicken pox lovely?" the doctor said. "All this time, the last four and a half years, I've been working on blown-apart . . . well, never mind. The war. Isn't chicken pox lovely? Just a boy with chicken pox." He sighed. "You'll have to process through the rest, get your bank of shots. Put the boy's shirt back on and keep it on so the spots don't show."

"Thank you," Mother said again.

"You have one more problem."

"What's that?"

"At the ship. There are inspectors at the ship and they may kick up a fuss if they see he has spots. The captain of the ship has final say and he may not let you on if he thinks there will be trouble with the inspectors."

"The captain?"

"Yes. He would be the one to talk to. The captain." The doctor looked at me and smiled for the first time. "It's so lovely, chicken pox. Thank you for letting me see them."

And Mother put my shirt on and dragged me and Dog in for shots.

Six

When we finished with the shots—I cried some but held it back when I was given a large sucker—Mother took me back to the hotel. She left me in the room for a short bit, then came back up from the front desk.

"I'm going to have to go out, Punkin," she told me. "Maybe for the evening. I have to go see the captain of the ship and talk to him."

I knew what it was all about. "So we can go."

"Yes. I want you to stay here in the room and the old woman who made the nice soup for you will watch you. Be good for her, will you?"

I thought of Clara back in Chicago. "Does she drink red wine and listen to the soap operas on the radio?"

"I don't know, but she seems very nice and we have to do this . . ."

Mother was moving as she spoke, in and out of the tiny bath alcove—there was not a bath but only a toilet and a small sink—getting ready to go. She pulled her sweater and slacks off, laid them over the foot of the bed, and selected a dark purple skirt from a suitcase. She swore quietly and shook the wrinkles out of the skirt.

"Goddamn—it's all wrinkled. Well, it will have to do."

It was fun to watch her dress because it changed her so much. Before Uncle Casey came to live with us I used to watch her come home from the war plant all tired and with smudges of dirt on her cheeks from the machinery she ran to make bullets. She would set up a mirror on the kitchen table and after a quick bath put her makeup on, dress in a sweater and skirt, and turn into a completely different woman—glamorous and so beautiful that wherever she walked men would stop and watch her.

She did that now. She checked her nails but did nothing to them, then a little here and a little there, combed her long blonde hair so the waves and curls fell just right, lipstick just so and blotted on a piece of toilet paper, some mascara, and she looked just like a movie star in a cigarette ad for Lucky Strikes. Then a garter belt and a pair of stockings, twisting to make sure they were straight before finally standing with her back to me.

"Are they all right?"

"Up and down," I said. It was part of our ritual before she went out. We'd done it for years, through most of the war. I was sitting on the small bed. The springs squeaked when I moved and I wondered if the old woman would let me jump up and down on it when Mother was gone.

"They took me halfway through the war," she said smiling, "and only one run." I remembered the run. It came when she bumped against the corner of a chair and a small upholstery nail had caught the nylon and pulled it. She had nearly cried, and she patched them with clear nail polish and somehow they'd made it through all this time.

With her seams straight she pulled on a short-sleeved sweater, adjusted it just so, restraightened her hair, and gave me a kiss that left lipstick on my cheek.

"How do I look?"

"Like a million," I said, and she did, too, but I didn't want her to go out because I knew that she was going to be with the captain and I didn't know the captain and I didn't want to know him. I thought of asking her if I would have to call the captain Uncle, but it didn't seem right and so I didn't. She went to the hallway and called down for the old Chinese woman to come up and left me in the room.

"My name Ty Lee," the old woman told me. "We play Chinese game while wait for mother."

She had a wooden radio under one arm and for a moment I thought it would be like Clara again and that she would just sit and listen to the radio, but I was wrong.

Beneath the other arm she had a folded case that opened out into a board with dice and pieces that moved and she set this on the bed.

She plugged the radio in and set it by the window, turned it on and waited for the tubes to warm up, and then tuned it to a station that was playing swing music.

"Benny," she said, smiling, waving her finger in time to the music. "Benny good. Now play. Make smart."

The game seemed to be simple at first. There were two dice and each time you shook them there would be a number to count on the dice and you would move several pieces to different squares. It only took me a couple of minutes to learn to count the dots on the dice and move my pieces. I didn't really understand what I was doing until Ty Lee showed me how to move first one piece and then another to block certain areas of the board and then it rapidly became too complicated for me. The ultimate idea was to control the board and not let the other pieces move, but there were so many ways to move your own pieces to block them that I couldn't keep up and after finding my level Ty Lee played so that I would always understand and we played for two or three hours.

Somewhere in the middle a Chinese man came up to the room.

He was carrying a tray of hot liquid—the same kind Ty Lee had given me the day before—and some small biscuits. We took a break and listened to music and looked out the window at all the Chinese people on the street, and we drank the soup and ate the biscuits. They had some snappy taste to them.

"The biscuits are good, but they burn my tongue," I said and Ty Lee nodded. I was propped on the pillow end of the bed and trying hard not to spill the drink. The cups were very small and did not have handles.

"That ginger. Ginger biscuits. Good for little white belly." She patted my stomach and turned and spoke in Chinese to the man and they both laughed. "Always eat ginger for little white belly. Ginger and rice and tea. Keep belly soft."

"I'll tell Mother," I said and wondered why it was good to have a soft stomach, but before I could ask we went back to playing. It was not long before my eyes started to close and Ty Lee put the board away. She sat next to me on the bed and sang a song in Chinese that went up and down and all around and put me sound asleep.

"Punkin, Punkin, wake up."

I rolled over on the bed and opened my eyes. Mother was standing near the bed. To her side and slightly behind her stood a man in a dark suit. I saw white rings on the cuff of the suit and knew that meant he was in the navy. I looked around the room and saw that the Chinese lady was gone.

"Where's Ty Lee?"

"I let her go, Punkin. This is Captain Pederson. He's the captain of the ship we're going to be on. You have to get up now, Punkin, we have to go to the ship."

Her breath smelled of beer and something stronger and she looked a little mussed. I saw lipstick on the captain's cheek, but I didn't say anything about it. I rubbed my eyes. "What time is it?"

"It's the middle of the night. Come on, Punkin. There's a cab waiting. We have to sneak on the boat."

"Ship," the captain said, and I saw when he spoke that he was close to drunk. He weaved slightly. He was a little taller than Mother and he had wide shoulders and short hair. He had a hat in his hands with a white top on it. "It's a ship—not a boat."

"Yes. Well . . . come on, Punkin. Wake up and help me help you."

She left me in my pajamas and put a coat around me. The captain took a woolen blanket from the bed and went to the door.

"We have to play a little game, Punkin. We're going to put you on the ship tonight and we have to sneak past some people that would keep us from going. So we're going to wrap you in the blanket from the hotel and get you to a special little room on the ship."

"Cabin." The captain stood by the door. "Not room, cabin . . ."

"Yes, cabin. Anyway, I have to leave you there, Punkin, for the rest of tonight and then tomorrow I will come on the ship. Do you see what I mean?"

"Is it because of my spots?"

"Yes. There are some rules about anybody with spots leaving the country and if they see you we won't be able to leave with the ship tomorrow. So we'll hide you on the ship tonight, and tomorrow I will come on as if there weren't anybody with me."

"I see."

"You'll have to stay in the cabin alone," Mother said. "Even after we get going because nobody is supposed to be there. So you'll have to be quiet and take orders."

"Is it like the war?"

"Yes. You have to be a soldier."

"Sailor," the captain said, smiling. He had the blanket over his shoulder and I liked his smile and hoped that I would not have to call him Uncle. "He has to be a sailor. I command a troopship. We haul soldiers—but we're sailors."

"Soldier," Mother said, her voice stronger. "His father is a soldier."

"Ah—well, then. Yes. Of course. A soldier."

He had some kind of accent that made me think of my Norwegian grandmother and I was going to ask if he knew her, but before I could say any more we were out and down the stairs, the captain in front with his hat on now and Mother carrying me.

Outside there was a taxi waiting and we drove through quiet streets to a place shrouded in thick fog, where we got out, Mother still carrying me. I couldn't see anything but sensed a large shape near us—the ship—and there was the rumble of engines, the sounds of water lapping and machinery clanking.

"Wait for us," the captain told the cabdriver. Then he turned to me and wrapped me in the blanket so that I was in a tube that he threw over his shoulder. I didn't see anything but darkness for a time.

We crossed some clunking wood—it moved a bit and I could feel him shift his weight and grab at a handrail.

"It's down quite a ways to the water, isn't it?" Mother asked. I heard the heels of her pumps clatter on wood.

"No talk now. Later."

Suddenly we entered a brightly lit area—the light came in the end of the blanket tube and made me squint—and it seemed there was the sound of big engines all around us, close and loud in a low thrumming that filled my body with vibration. We bumped along for a good bit more, went around some tight turns—on one of them he bumped my head against a corner that didn't give—and then we stopped.

I was unrolled and put on my feet and saw that we were in a small room, a cabin. It was completely white, painted white in every nook and corner—floor, walls, ceiling, all of it. On one wall there were two bunks—both white—and bolted to the wall at the end of the bunks was a white table in front of which stood a white metal chair. On another wall was a white metal toilet and next to that a white metal sink with one faucet and a mirror. Over the door was a light bulb—the only light in the room—and it was surrounded by a white wire cage.

On each bunk there was a rolled mattress and a dark blue blanket—the only break from white in the whole cabin—folded with two sheets and a pillow and pillowcase.

"This is your cabin, soldier," the captain said, and I looked to see if he was smiling but he wasn't.

"Can I have the top bunk?"

"Either one. We'll leave you now. There will be an inspection at 0900 . . ."

"Let me make his bed," Mother said, but the captain shook his head.

"No. He's in the navy now—he has to do it alone."

He took her arm and guided her out of the cabin and closed the door. She watched over her shoulder, smiling, and I stood holding Dog, listening to the hum of the engines around me, watching them leave, and wondering if soldiers were allowed to be tucked in at all.

I turned to the bunk and saw there was a little ladder on the end. I climbed onto the bare springs of the top bunk and unrolled the mattress. Then I spread the sheets out in a rumpled mass, did the same with the blanket of coarse wool with an anchor in a white circle in the middle, and stuffed the pillow in the pillowcase.

With everything more or less in the right place I lay out and pulled the blanket and sheet over me and dropped back on the pillow.

The room was so bright, stark white-bright, that I didn't think I could close my eyes. But something from the rhythm of the engines took me, the hum or vibration in the bunk, and I was asleep in minutes with Dog jammed in next to my neck.

Seven

I had no idea of day or night when I awakened or why my eyes were suddenly open. There was no porthole in the cabin and nothing changed—all light and sound was exactly as when I had gone to sleep. But I awakened and sat up—my head barely cleared the overhead ceiling—and clambered down the ladder to pee.

When I flushed the toilet with the small lever on the wall I suddenly felt the ship move and I thought I had done something wrong and ran back to the bunk. But that did not stop the movement and it felt as if we were going at first sideways, then backward, then forward, all at once. It was a very small movement but it was there, and I grabbed the side rail of the bunk to hold on and wondered what would happen if I were to open the door and just see if there was anybody to ask about the movement. I thought about what if we were on the ocean now and what if there were a Jap sub and they hadn't heard the war was over and they torpedoed us and I wouldn't even know it, inside the white little cabin, until the water came roaring through the door . . .

The door opened suddenly and Mother came in, followed by

a man with short blond hair and large blue eyes almost as big as Mother's.

"Hello, Punkin." She looked fresh and new with slacks and a sweater and her hair combed back.

"Is it day?" I asked.

"Yes. It's six in the morning and we are just now leaving the dock. Isn't it exciting?"

"Where is the captain?"

She shook her head and looked at the man, but he didn't seem to care what we talked about. He smiled at me.

"Hi," he said. "My name is Harding. I'm a corpsman."

"What's that?"

"In the army they call us medics—do you know what that is?"

"Sure. My dad is in the army. He killed lots of Germans . . ."

"That's all right, Punkin. The war is over."

"Well, still . . . he killed lots of Germans."

"Yes, but Seaman Harding isn't here for that. He's here to help you."

"You are?" I asked him.

"I sure am. This cabin is part of the dispensary, and I'm going to be your friend while you're down here. Is there anything I can get for you?"

"A coke?"

He shook his head. "That I can't do, but I'll bet I could find some lemonade. Would that do?"

"It would be perfect," Mother said, cutting in. "And he thanks you, don't you, Punkin?"

"Thank you very much."

"No problem."

He left the cabin and Mother came close to the bunk and hugged me. "I sure missed you, Punkin."

"Where is your stuff? Aren't you going to be here with me?"

She shook her head. "I can't. I'm not even supposed to come visit you in case I carry some of your germs out with me."

"I don't feel like I have any germs."

"I know, Punkin, but that's how the rules are. The captain said I could come down here once a day, but I'm not supposed to hug you or anything." She hugged me again. "I'll bring things when I come to help you pass the time and it won't take long—maybe only ten days. Seaman Harding will be with you all the time—he sleeps in the next cabin—and as soon as the spots are gone you can come up and stay in my cabin with me. It won't be any time at all, you'll see."

Which wasn't true.

I was in the cabin only nine days, but they seemed like several years, seemed like the rest of my life because Mother couldn't come down each day. For the first week of sailing she was so sick she could barely walk, and the three times I saw her—green, weak, leaning over the commode every minute or so—she could do little more than survive. She tried, but in the end she could do nothing but stay in the bunk in her cabin for that first week and throw up in a bucket provided by the crew.

I, on the other hand, became more and more healthy and by the third or fourth day was close to bouncing off the walls of the small cabin.

Harding tried. He was very nice and brought me food on metal trays and sat with me and read comic books to me until he looked sick if I said Captain Marvel or Superman. He used some purple stuff on my spots so that in six days they were gone except for the purple marks.

The daily routine was exactly the same. Each morning at five-thirty—I still had no idea of time except that Harding would tell me what time it was—Harding came in and tapped me on the shoulder.

He always had a cup of hot chocolate and as soon as I had peed and washed my face and hands I sat at the table and drank the hot chocolate while he used a magnifying glass to look at the spots.

"Much better," he said each morning, nodding. "Much, much better."

"Could you read me a comic book?" I would ask, and each morning he would shake his head.

"Later. You have to have chow and clean for inspection."

So he would bring me breakfast, which I quickly learned to call "chow," because I thought it was the military thing to do and I thought how good it would be to tell my father I ate chow on the boat. The breakfast was always the same. Scrambled powdered eggs fried in grease with two pieces of dry toast, a small bowl of oatmeal with milk mixed from powder that still had lumps in it and no sugar—all of which I had to eat before proceeding to the next step: cleaning the cabin for the captain's inspection.

I would try to make my bed tight as per Harding's instructions, with the right kinds of hospital corners so it would bounce a quarter and the pillow just so. Then I'd take a damp cloth and wipe down the entire cabin, walls, bunks, chair, table, and floor and, especially, the ledge over the door.

It was never good enough.

When the captain came down the first time for inspection I looked behind him for Mother and when she didn't show I smiled at him, remembering how nice he had been the night he came back to the room with Mother to carry me to the ship.

He had changed completely. Where he had seemed happy, he now scowled, and Harding made me stand at attention to the side of the door while the captain completed his inspection.

He wore white gloves and his hands probed and flew and rubbed everywhere, and no matter how well I cleaned, no matter how I dampened the cleaning rag in the small sink on the wall and stood on the chair to scrub over the door, the gloves always came away from the ledge over the door with dirt on them, little smudges of gray, and he would turn to me and the scowl would deepen.

Then he would walk to the bunk and drop a quarter and the quarter—the goddamn thing, as I thought of it—would just lie flat and dead and he would shake his head and pick up the quarter and hold the finger out to show the dirt from above the door and shake his head and say:

"Not good enough. Not nearly good enough. See to it, Harding."

"Aye, aye, sir," Harding would say and look distressed, and the captain would leave and I would sit back at the table while Harding went around the cabin cleaning it again, but it didn't help.

In the middle of the day Harding brought me a meal on a tray. Again, it never varied. Meat with some gravy and runny powdered mashed potatoes, all in quantities impossible for me to eat so that even Harding, who insisted I clean everything up, had to admit I couldn't get it down and flushed what was remaining down the toilet. Or head, as I was told to call it. Chow for food, overhead for ceiling, rack for bunk, deck for floor, head for toilet, bulkhead for wall—Harding helped me memorize the right names.

In the afternoon Harding left me to myself while he worked in the dispensary next door and I read comic books, except that I could not read and had to just look at pictures. Captain Marvel and Superman and Donald Duck were my favorites and I would go over them time and again. After he worked Harding came in to sit with me and check the purple spots again to make sure they were working right. Then he would read to me out of the comic books and I would try to memorize the stories so that later I could look at the pictures and follow along.

Then it would be the end of the day and I would get into the bunk—rack—to go to sleep. Strangely, I did not have any trouble sleeping. The rumble of the engines, the movement of the ship—it was never rough—seemed to lull me and I rarely lay awake for more than a few moments before my eyes would close and I would be gone.

This lasted for five days.

On the afternoon of the fifth day there was a knock on the cabin door and Harding opened it to see a soldier standing there in uniform. He had a Hershey bar in his hand.

"For the boy," he said. "The word's out that he can't leave the cabin."

"Thank you," Harding said and looked at me. I nodded and thanked the man and went forward to get the candy bar.

Half an hour later another soldier came and left another candy bar, a Baby Ruth, and then another with a Butterfinger, and it went that way for the rest of the fifth day until finally, just before evening chow, Harding stood from the table.

"Now wait a minute." Harding held up his hand.

There was another soldier at the door holding out a bottle of 7-Up, which I took to add to the growing pile of wealth I had stored on the bottom bunk.

"What's the matter?" The soldier's eyes were wide, innocent.

"That makes eight of you to come in with stuff for the kid," Harding said. "What's going on?"

"He's locked in." The soldier shrugged. "We just want to make it easier for him."

"Right." Harding's voice was skeptical. "Let's step out in the alleyway." He moved with the soldier—after I had thanked him and snagged the 7-Up for the bunk—and partially closed the hatch, but I could still hear by standing close to the back of the hinge.

"What the hell is going on here?"

"Have you seen the kid's mother?" the soldier asked.

"Yeah—so what?"

"Jesus, man, she's a knockout. It's a long ride to the goddamn

Philippines. What's the matter with trying to meet a good-looking woman by bringing a candy bar to her kid?"

Harding sighed. "Look, I'm responsible for the kid. Don't screw things up, right?"

"Hell, how are we hurting him? We're giving him candy and pop to help him pass the time. What does that hurt? Did you see her tits? Goddamn, man."

"Shut the hell up." Harding hissed. "The kid is right here."

"Hell, what does he know?"

"How many men are there waiting to bring things down for him?"

"Shit, *I* don't know. There are two hundred soldiers on the ship, heading back to occupy Japan. Most of them want to meet her. There's a list in the dayroom on the top deck. Must be sixty, seventy men."

"Christ. Look, he's a good kid trying hard to do this right and he thinks you're all great because you're soldiers."

"Jesus."

"Exactly."

And I heard the soldier move off down the alleyway. Harding came back in and I sat on the bunk with candy bars and bottles of pop and comic books and wondered about hell. Like would I go to hell if I took the candy bars and pop because my mother had nice tits and the soldiers wanted to meet her and do what Uncle Casey did? Or if I gave the candy bars and pop back to the soldiers so they couldn't meet Mother would it keep me from going to hell? Or if I gave the stuff back to the soldiers but some of them met Mother anyway would it be the same as if I had kept the candy and pop? And in that case couldn't I just keep the stuff and not help Mother meet any soldiers who liked her tits and not go to hell?

Harding read to me out of a comic book, but for once I wasn't listening. I was too busy working on the problem and I finally decided it was all right to keep the candy as long as I didn't help

Mother meet any men who would be like Uncle Casey. And that set me to wondering if I had room in the cabin to store all the stuff the soldiers brought or if the captain would even let me keep it.

It was the first day that I didn't become bored. The soldiers kept coming, bringing things, and I kept taking them until finally it was time for bed. I staggered onto the top bunk holding new comic books and candy bars and prepared to settle in for the night when the door opened and Mother came in.

"Hi, Punkin," she said. Her face was green and she was hanging on to the edge of the opening. "Are you doing all right?"

"Fine . . ."

"What's all the candy and pop?"

"Soldiers bring it to me. Here, would you like a bite of Baby Ruth?"

She seemed to hang in the opening for a split second, then wheeled and threw up in the commode bolted to the wall. Harding came in with a pan and a damp cloth. He wiped her forehead and held it while she was sick, then went with her into the companionway and back up to her cabin. He returned in a few minutes and helped me get ready for sleep.

"Harding?" I asked.

"Yes."

"Did you help Mother because you like her or because she's got nice tits?"

He choked a bit, then recovered. "What made you ask that?"

"Oh, I don't know."

"Were you hearing some things you shouldn't have heard?"

I shook my head. "I don't think so."

"You'd better go to sleep."

"You didn't answer my question."

"Go to sleep—that's an order."

"Aye, aye, sir."

Eight

 "Punkin, come on, hurry up—a plane is going to come down."

It was midafternoon on the ninth day. Harding had decided all the spots were gone and that I would be able to leave the dispensary the next morning and Mother had come bursting into the cabin.

"What . . . ," Harding started. He'd been trying without success to get me interested in a Wonder Woman comic book and he jumped when she came in.

"Right now. It's circled three times trying to get it right. A big one. And the captain is stopping the ship."

As if on cue the rumble of engines slowed and the movement lost its direction as the ship slowed. At the same time a buzzer sounded in the dispensary and I heard the captain's voice on a speaker:

"Harding—report with emergency kit to boat davit three."

"Aye, aye, sir," Harding answered, yelling at the speaker. He ran into the dispensary and came out with an olive-drab canvas bag—all in seconds—and ran away from us and up the alleyway.

"Come on." Mother grabbed my hand and dragged me after her.

All this time, except for peeking out of the open hatchway once when Harding left it open, I had never been outside the cabin. I had no idea where to go, where I was, how to get anywhere except by following, and that presented problems.

I had been dressed in pajamas for most of the week, but Harding took them to be washed and left me with a pair of khaki shorts about six sizes too big with an old army belt to hold them up and a small men's T-shirt that was so large it nearly dragged on the floor; my own clothing was packed away. I kept tripping on my clothes, trying to hold them off the deck, and barely kept up as Mother trotted ahead down alleyways and through hatchways, up a steep stairway—which I knew enough to call a ladder—and out, suddenly, into dazzling sunlight.

I was blinded. Even the white in the cabin with the light on could not have prepared me for this sudden explosion of light. It seemed to come from all around, inside my head—a blast of brightness. I reeled back against the wall and covered my eyes, opened them a little, closed them, and finally eased them open enough to see.

Blue.

All around was the clean, turquoise blue of the Pacific that went out and out, up in a dish to meet the blue of the sky. There was no wind and the ocean seemed to be almost flat, although I could make out low swells that rolled beneath the ship.

I could hear a great clamoring and rattling, and I moved to the handrail to see what caused the noise.

Toward the front of the boat but on our side, where the hatchway from the dispensary came onto the deck, there were men beginning to lower a boat to the water on ropes. The boat was bouncing against the side of the ship, clattering chains as it did. Harding ran to the rail and jumped over the side into the swinging boat and it began to lower, but the man working the drop misjudged the height of the swells and let it go too fast toward the end so that the boat dropped the last seven or eight feet to the water with a huge splash.

There was much swearing and gesturing from the men in the boat back up to the man working the winch. Harding was driven to the bottom of the boat and I saw him open the bag to check his gear.

The air was filled with a great frantic feeling that I didn't understand. The plane was still flying and didn't seem to be coming down soon. Harding looked up at us once, smiled at me—or Mother—and went back to his bag. They unhooked the ropes holding the boat to the ship and started an engine in the rear and moved away. Somebody threw several sets of rope ladders over the sides.

All of this hadn't taken three or four minutes. I was still half dazed and dizzy from coming out of confinement and into the outside so suddenly.

I heard the plane then.

It did not sound bad, the way I had heard planes sound in movies when they were in trouble, sputtering and rattling or whining in to crash when a Jap or kraut shot it down. This sounded even, full. It came over the ship from the rear and jumped into view overhead, silver and bright and clean looking. It was very low, just over the height of the ship, and when it banked to circle I saw that the two propellers on the right wing were not turning. They were frozen in position, or seemed to be, and the plane kept circling to the right in a wide turn that took it around out of sight past the stern of the ship. In a moment it came back around again into sight over the bow and it circled that way for ten or fifteen more minutes while the ship sat still on the flat sea and the boat with Harding and the two other sailors held position next to us.

When the plane was in sight I watched it, but when it circled back over us I had a moment to see other things and I thought at first how big the ship seemed to be. I leaned out over the rail to see how long it was and Mother snatched me back.

"Don't do that!" She held my arm. "You'll fall and the sharks will get you."

"What sharks?"

"They follow the ship to get the garbage we throw away—back by the rear end."

"Stern," I said, Harding's lessons coming to the fore. "The rear end is the stern." I looked for sharks but didn't see any. Then again, I couldn't see the stern, either—it seemed to be a mile away.

"Just stay next to me."

By now the deck was filling with soldiers and off-duty sailors, coming to watch the crash. Most of them were in uniform, some in pants and T-shirts, and many—dozens—seemed to know Mother and worked hard to get next to her so that in moments I was jammed back against the bulkhead wall of the cabins and couldn't see anything. I tried to wiggle through but there wasn't any room, and I was just thinking of getting down to crawl when I felt strong hands under my armpits and I was raised up and up until I was looking into the smiling face of a man with black, wavy hair with oil in it and brown eyes. He was wearing a set of khakis with corporal stripes on the sleeve.

"Come on, kid, get up and ride." He lifted me up—I had never felt anything so strong—and dropped me on his shoulders so my legs were around his neck and I was looking down on the black hair and could see over everybody.

"Thanks," I said, but he was looking at Mother. She had turned to him and saw me sitting on his shoulders and when she saw me she smiled, then dropped her eyes to the corporal's face.

"Thank you. There are so many men around here, I thought I'd lost him." There were men pressing from all sides, most of them trying to talk to Mother, and they seemed to push Mother toward the corporal so she was looking up into his eyes.

"It's because of you," the corporal said. "I don't blame them."

Mother blushed but didn't look away, and I tried to remember if the corporal was one of the men who brought me candy because Mother had nice tits, but I couldn't place him.

"My name's Havermeyer," the corporal said. "The boy was getting backed against the wall. I thought I'd help him."

Mother started to say more, or at least I think she did. Her lips parted and she licked them slightly and seemed on the edge of a word. I felt Havermeyer lean forward, but somebody nearby yelled suddenly.

"She's coming down!"

Mother turned to the rail and I looked up to see that the plane, just coming around on another circle, had changed its flight. It moved straight away this time, until it was a speck in the sky, then turned in a shallow, huge turn to the right and started back.

Lower.

It seemed to flare out in some way, as a bird does in landing. The nose came up and the plane slowed as it came toward us. It dropped lower and lower until it seemed to be just above the wave and hardly moving at all.

All the men were silent and I felt myself holding my breath, waiting for it to drop the . . . last . . . little . . . bit.

It hit with a crack we could easily hear from the ship—a great, hissing snap of a sound. A giant spray of water flew into the air, obscuring the plane completely and for part of a second I thought it had sunk, driven itself down into the blue water.

Then it came out of the spray in a huge, leaping bound, skipping like a rock on water, seeming to float in the air for minutes before settling back into another splash. This time it did not rise but skittered across the water, flat on its belly, sliding sideways but toward the ship.

The tail broke off just as it hit the second time and debris could be seen flying through the air, junk and seats and suitcases and, I thought, people—but I could have been wrong—and it stopped.

Absolutely stopped. The silver plane on the blue, blue water stopped dead near enough the ship to see movement in the cockpit and in two or three seconds the door on the side popped open and people came out onto the wing.

"Shit, it's women and kids," one of the men said, and I believe that was the first word I'd heard uttered since the plane started down.

With the tail broken off the plane began to fill immediately and went down by the rear so that the nose came up slightly. I thought it would sink before the people could get out—I found later it was a planeload of military dependents coming back from Hawaii—but the wings seemed to stop the downward motion and hold the plane up for a few moments more.

The man had been right. All the survivors seemed to be women and kids and some of them were hurt—I could see from the ship the red of blood. They were all wearing Mae West life vests and the wings were awash. They started to jump off into the water, some women holding babies, and the boat from the ship was halfway over to the plane and I thought they would be all right, except for the ones who were hurt in the crash, when somebody in back of me yelled.

"The sharks! Look at the goddamn sharks!"

There were many of them, as Mother had said, following the ship and from above you could see their gray shapes, like huge gray bullets just beneath the surface arrowing for the wreck.

Some of the men started to yell, but it was too far to the plane for the sound to carry and there was nothing they could have done anyway. The people were in the water, and now the boat seemed to be moving so very slowly, crawling toward them. I could see Harding in the bow, leaning forward. He seemed to be straining toward the heads bobbing in the water, pulling the boat ahead.

When the sharks hit them, at first it did not seem such a very terrible thing.

It was so far and I was watching one person by the wing and he bobbed two or three times as something beneath the water grabbed at him and then he was gone, down and gone, and I did not think it bothered me except that I found I was squeezing the top of Havermeyer's head without meaning to, squeezing so hard he reached up and pushed my arms up to relieve the pressure.

"Easy . . ."

With the first one or two hits the rest of the people realized what was happening and they panicked, thrashing at the water, but it did no good. The sharks were into them fully now, tearing at them, and one after another they went down. Some were being jerked at even when the boat arrived and Harding reached for them. And then I saw the woman.

There were many people in the water. Thirty or forty, at least, and many of them were being hit at the same time, but I saw a woman with a baby and she tried to save the baby.

The wing of the plane was awash, but still there was a little showing and the woman tried to put the baby on the wing so it would be safe and all the time the sharks were hitting her, jerking her down, and she kept putting the baby back on the wing, setting it there so it would be safe. But they took her, finally, took her down, and the baby rolled off the wing and they got the baby as well. Swirl and gone.

"Jesus fucking Christ," I heard Mother say, her voice even. "The sons of bitches, the dirty sons of bitches . . ." And I saw then that she had a camera, had brought a small box camera with her onto the deck. It hung by the little handle in her hand, but she wasn't taking any pictures and I was glad. I didn't want pictures of this, didn't want to watch even now except that I couldn't turn away.

Harding and the other men were among the people now and pulling them into the boat as fast as they could. Some had legs missing, and I could see the blood and damage from where I sat on Havermeyer's shoulders. I didn't want to look because I knew I would dream, dream of all of it, but I couldn't stop looking, either.

A second boat had been lowered while the first was making its way to the plane and it arrived just as the plane slid beneath the water, and four men in the second boat began pulling at people. Sometimes they had to pull against the sharks who were jerking on the other end. One man, out by the end of the wing—it might have been the pilot or copilot—suddenly turned end for end, a bloody trunk sticking in the air as the sharks tore off the bottom half.

It was possible now to see the sharks, their fins and sometimes their tails, as they thrashed among the swimmers. And then they were done and the boats had all they would get, alive or dead.

They started back for the ship. I could see Harding working on people in the bottom of the boat, and as they came closer I could hear the people screaming, some of them so high that it seemed to cut the air and go into me. High-pitched screams, tight and high mixed with spit.

"Volunteers aft." It was the captain's voice on a loudspeaker. "Anybody with first-aid knowledge report aft to help when the boats come aboard, please."

Many of the men left the rail and some of them moved toward the rear of the ship. Mother turned to me.

"I'm going to go help, Punkin. You stay out of the way . . ."

And she was gone, moving down the walkway on the side of the ship. I squirmed a little and Havermeyer put me down.

"I'm not sure your mother would want you to be back there with her," he said.

But that didn't mean anything. It wasn't an order and he didn't hold me, so I moved off with the men.

The sea was flat and the boats came back faster than they had gone to the site of the wreck. By the time we arrived at the stern where the ropes hung down they were already hooked up and being raised to the level of the deck on the ship.

The noise now was deafening. Many of them were screaming, especially some children that had their legs torn off, and I looked over the rail down into the boats as they came up.

Harding was covered with blood, as were the other men and most of the plane's passengers. I could not believe there could be that much blood inside people. It sprayed from wounds, pulsed from them, oozed and dripped and flowed, so that the boats seemed to be awash with blood. It had probably mixed with sea-water but it looked pure, red, and it sloshed back and forth in the bottoms of the boats.

As soon as the lifeboats were on the deck, settling into the storage cradles, men reached in and lifted people out. Some had brought blankets from the cabins and these had been spread for the injured.

There were only four men among them. All the rest—twenty-three of them—were women and children, and at least two-thirds of them had been hit by the sharks.

Some could not be saved. So much blood had been lost that several were dead as they were lifted out of the boat. Others died while I watched.

One boy about my size with brown hair was holding his stomach, or where his stomach had been, and he looked at me, into my eyes, and the light went out and the eyes lost focus and he died. I had never seen blood this way, blood and worse, and I was sick. But I could not stop watching. I threw up, but still did not turn away.

Harding was everywhere. He went from one to the next and other men helped as they could, but Mother kneeled next to Harding and began to work with him and he looked at her and nodded and from then on she stayed with him.

His bag was full of bandages and a drug he injected into some that were torn more than others—I think to help with the pain.

Some he stitched, pulling wounds together and sewing them with a needle right there in the open on the deck, dusting them with some powder, and then Mother would bandage from bandages and compresses in the bag and they would move on to another.

Some they did not help.

Mother stopped near one woman whose side and most of her insides seemed to be gone. Harding looked at her and shook his head.

"But . . . ," Mother started to say something.

Harding shook his head again and the woman saw him and there was fear in her eyes and Mother took her hand. She was young and had black hair plastered to her head with blood and seawater and large, dark eyes full of fear and I think Mother would have stayed with her except that Harding caught her eye.

"I need you. Bad."

And she let the woman's hand go and the woman lasted some more time and then died. Only when she died did I realize that she looked like the boy who had watched me as he died, and I wondered if she had been his mother.

I do not know how long they worked on the deck. Each time Harding and Mother and the soldiers finished helping somebody other soldiers would use a stretcher and take them below to the dispensary. Finally there were no more and Mother and Harding stood.

Mother looked as bad as he did—her hair, clothes, everything red with blood. She spat something and turned sideways and threw up over the rail. Harding stopped next to her.

"It will be worse below," he said. "Can you help me? There are so many women and children. If I had a woman helping me it might calm them . . ."

She did not say anything, but nodded and followed him, and the men moved apart for them. I slipped in blood and fell on the deck but followed, wiping my hands on my shorts, moving down through the alleyways and stairs to the dispensary.

Nine

It was easy to find the way back to the dispensary. In the rush of all that was going on I was completely ignored, and I followed Mother and Harding and several other men who went to help.

The dispensary was a small room next to my cabin. There was a metal table in the dispensary itself and an injured woman was on the table, her head rocking from side to side slowly and her teeth making a gnashing sound that I could hear all the way out in the alleyway.

Everywhere there were wounded people—women and children. They were on the deck, in the alleyway, back into my cabin—in the bunks and on the floor in my cabin—and it seemed that all of them were bleeding.

Those who hadn't actually been injured in the crash or by the sharks seemed to be numbed with shock and sat against the cabin walls and in the alleyway wrapped in dark blue blankets, and I stood and stared at them.

"We have to tie some of the vessels off or many of them won't make it," I heard Harding say. I had been standing in the alleyway looking at the carnage in my cabin. One boy of ten or twelve sat huddled in a corner and seemed to be staring through me, the walls, the decks, the ship, everything.

"I'll need you to help," Harding continued. He was talking to Mother. "You have to stay on your feet."

She nodded but said nothing.

"Without throwing up because you'll be wearing a mask."

Again she nodded.

"Can you give shots?"

"Teach me. I'll do it." Her voice sounded hollow, far away.

He took a metal tray with glass hypodermics and some needles from a case on the wall and found a bottle. "This is morphine. Give each of the worst injured ones this much—this line right here. Hurry as much as you can. Don't worry about rubbing with alcohol or any of that. Just go along and do it while I prepare for surgery. Get some of those men to hold them down while you give the shots and then get back in here as soon as you're done."

Mother came out of the dispensary with the hypodermic and the bottle and motioned to three soldiers who were standing waiting to help. I recognized two of them as having brought me candy or comic books.

"This one first . . ."

She moved from one to the next of those most seriously injured and gave shots, and I thought she must have learned somewhere to do it so well. The soldiers helped and talked and held the people, and Mother would give them morphine, and even those in really bad shape—and some of them died while waiting—seemed to become quiet with the morphine, almost as soon as Mother put the needle in.

I couldn't get into my cabin—it was jammed full—so I stood in the alleyway so that I could see into the dispensary and I saw things I didn't want to see there, but still I could not quit looking.

Harding wasn't a doctor—corpsmen and medics are not even nurses, I found out later—but he was all they had, the wounded people, and he must have known things from the war because he cut and tied and sutured and at one incredible point used a small saw to remove the rest of a leg that was mostly gone from a shark bite. Through it all Mother stood with him, handing him things, helping the people on the tables, talking to them while Harding worked, and sometimes holding them down so that he *could* work.

Once the captain came and stood, shaking his head but saying nothing, and shortly after that a Filipino steward came down with a pot of hot coffee and cups and a bucket of soup. The soup he gave to the soldiers to give to the wounded, and he gave the coffee to Mother and Harding. Mother lifted her mask to take a sip of coffee with a hand that was completely caked with blood and tissue and in some way it looked delicate, feminine, a bloody pinky in the air as she sipped.

I do not know for certain the time they stopped, finally stopped. I had long before become tired of standing and slid down the wall, inured enough to the gore and screaming and crying to close my eyes in exhaustion and sleep in short bits.

I opened them in silence, a sudden quiet, and I looked in to see Mother and Harding looking at each other across an empty table. Harding pulled his mask down and Mother did the same, and I saw that except for a white square where the mask had been she was completely dark, almost black, with blood that had dried on her face and clothing and in her hair.

Harding turned to a small sink on the wall and dampened a cloth and came around the table. He reached with the cloth and wiped Mother's face, small dabs at first, then wider circles, rewetting the rag and rinsing it out and working more until her face was clean and then he reached back and undid the barrette holding her hair. Her hair was dirty as well and she followed him to the sink, where he washed it. And when he was done he dried it with a clean towel.

She stood, just stood for all this. When her hair was dry he wrapped the towel around her head, and he held her cheeks and pulled her face to his and kissed her.

But it wasn't the Uncle Casey kind of kiss or a kiss because he liked her tits. It was just to be a friend, I think, the way Mother kissed me when she dried my hair sometimes. She didn't push him away but seemed to kiss him back.

"Take the kid back up to your cabin and get some sleep. You're out on your feet and we've done all we can."

"You still need help."

"Always. There are others, soldiers who will help. You get some sleep now—it's two in the morning."

"It is?"

"We've been almost eighteen hours working on them. Get some sleep. Then come back and help me again."

I stood up. All the soldiers were gone and the people on the bunks and the floor of my cabin seemed to be asleep, though some moaned and turned while they slept. I wanted to get Dog but he was in the top bunk and Harding had put two little girls up there, both torn up, and I didn't think it was right to disturb them. Besides, one of them was holding Dog and had blood all over him and I thought maybe it was time to give Dog up.

"How long have you been out here?" Mother came through the door and took my hand.

"Through all of it."

"It was terrible, wasn't it, Punkin? I'm sorry you had to see it."

"I saw the boy die and then the woman, too. They were looking right at me."

"It was awful."

All the time, she was leading me back up the passageway. I saw that it had been cleaned and wondered who had done it and then remembered the soldiers.

"We're going to the cabin I've been sleeping in," she said. "It's up on the deck . . ."

It was dark when we came on deck and the moon was up and made a silver line across the water. Mother stopped at the rail and took deep breaths of the cool night air that came along the side of the ship.

The water looked dark to me, dark and full of sharks and things that killed, and went on forever and I wondered if we would ever get to the Philippines and see Father.

"How far is it?" I asked.

"How far is what?" She held my hand tightly and looked down.

"To where we're going—to the Philippines. How far do we have to go?"

"Oh, Punkin, it's halfway around the world. About as far as you can go."

"I want to be back in Chicago."

She didn't say anything then but picked me up and hugged me and took me to her cabin. There were two bunks and she put me in the top bunk to go to sleep and climbed into the bottom one herself, after dropping her clothes down to a bra and panties and wiping off with a damp rag from the sink on the wall.

But I kept seeing things when I closed my eyes and couldn't sleep and climbed down and into bed with her, cuddled next to her side. She was already asleep, her breathing deep and even, but the smell of blood was still in the room, from her clothes and mine, which I was still wearing, and it took a long time for my eyes to close and stay closed and not make the pictures of the boats and the sharks and the screams and the woman putting her baby on the wing again and again while the sharks hit her.

Ten

Mother was a heroine after the crash and there was always a long line of men waiting to be with her wherever she happened to be.

"It's so embarrassing," she said to me once. "All these men want to talk to me . . ."

I could have told her the real reason but I didn't think it was right and besides, I was settling into the new shipboard life and finding that there were so many things to do and places to go that I rarely saw her during the day.

I was allowed to stay in Mother's cabin after the wreck. When I awakened that first morning she was gone and I faintly remembered her kissing me and telling me she had to go down to the dispensary and help Harding.

I was in new shorts and a different T-shirt and I wandered out on deck into the same dazzling blueness as it had been the day before. There was more wind so that whitecaps dotted the ocean. I saw some fish that seemed to be flying from one wave to the next. I watched them for a while and then realized I was starved. I hadn't eaten the entire day before and I was so hungry I could hardly stand.

I saw a group of soldiers by a large opening into the side of the upper deck and I went up to them.

"Is there a place where there is food?" I asked.

"Oh, look, it's the kid. Yeah, sure kid, come on, we'll get you food."

They walked across the deck a ways and down a series of ladders and I found we were in the galley, with tables and benches.

"They have food all the time, kid, because we eat in shifts. What do you want?"

The man talking to me was Havermeyer, who had come forward in the group when he saw me.

"Anything."

"You want soldier food?"

I nodded. "I'd like that." I wanted to be a soldier.

"Give the kid S.O.S.," he said to the cook, and the cook—he was a fat man with a mole on his nose—smiled and put a piece of toast on a tray and dumped some gray glop on it. Then Havermeyer gave me some milk in a cup, a fork, and a knife, and put me at the table.

"You tell your mom I fed you, right?"

I nodded and he moved off with the men, smiling. I set to eating. The food tasted salty but there were small chunks of meat in it and I ate it all, wiping the tray with my finger. I drank all the milk and put the tray in a metal window where the dirty trays were stacked and left the galley.

I did not remember for certain how to get to the top of the ship again, but I climbed all the up ladders I could and found myself coming out onto a little deck near the bridge, way above the main deck. The doorway was next to the room where they steered the ship and I saw the captain there.

"Ah, boy, released from your prison, are you?"

"Yes, sir."

"Good for you. Would you like to steer the ship?"

"I don't know how."

"Easy as pie. Jennings will help you. Give him a hand, Jennings."

"Aye, aye, sir." The man at the big brass wheel stood to the side and showed me how to steer and look at the compass on top of a pedestal. I had to stand on tiptoe to see the compass. "It's all points and numbers."

"That's so we can tell where we're going." The captain swung his arm toward the sea. "Otherwise we'd never find our way across the ocean."

"Is that what happened to the plane?"

"No. They had engine trouble and had to land." He looked at me. "Your mother was splendid, boy. Incredible. Many of them would have died if she hadn't helped."

"I saw a boy die and then I think his mother."

The captain wasn't listening to me. He was looking out of the windows at the sea. "Come through the whole goddamn war without a scratch, never even got fired at, and then these poor bastards . . ."

I steered for a little while, but it wasn't as exciting as it first looked and I left the bridge to find my way back down to the dispensary.

Mother was there with Harding, helping to change bandages and clean them. I watched and tried to help Mother, but when they took the bandages off I couldn't be there without getting sick so I decided to leave.

"You stay around here now," Mother said. She was holding a pan while Harding worked on a place on a woman's arm where everything was gone and like the plane wreck I didn't want to look but couldn't help looking. "I don't want you running around the ship."

"I'll get sick if I watch," I said. The woman they were working on was staring at the ceiling. There was no indication she felt anything. Her eyes were wide and flat and they didn't blink, just stared at the white ceiling.

"You have to help," Mother said and I thought she meant at the bandages and I started to try but she shook her head. "No. There's a little boy in your cabin with the others. His name is Jimmy and he lost his mother. Why don't you sit and talk to him for a while?"

I went into the cabin where I had been with chicken pox and found there were just two boys. One was small and he was sitting in a woman's lap, and I figured that was his mother. The other was about my age and he was sitting alone in the corner, staring at the floor.

"Hi." I squatted next to him and told him my name. "Are you Jimmy?"

He looked at me and I could see that he'd been crying—his eyes were deep red—but he didn't say anything or even nod.

"Mother says you're alone and need somebody. You want to go play up on deck? You can see the ocean and the other parts of the ship and the captain will let you steer if we go to the steering place."

I stood up and he did the same and followed me without talking or making any sign that he'd heard me. I moved through the companionways and up the ladders to the deck and out into the sun and he stayed with me and never said a word.

We went all over the ship, Jimmy and I. There were soldiers everywhere, sleeping on blankets with their shirts off, reading books in shady places, smoking and drinking beer out of brown bottles and cans that were shaped like bottles and had caps like bottles they had to open with a bottle opener. They were all nice to us and nobody made an effort to keep us from doing anything or going anyplace.

In the bow there was a curved place where you could crawl out and look back and down to the bow cutting the water and we watched dolphins—one of the soldiers told me what they were—swirling ahead of the ship. It seemed to move very fast through the water, though it was a slow ship, and I watched the dolphins, one over the other almost like my grandmother braiding her hair, one over one over one over until I realized that Jimmy wasn't watching with me.

He had settled down to the deck and was sitting with his back to the rail and was staring at the deck.

"Well, who wants to watch dolphins anyway," I said. "Would you like to steer the boat?"

And again he followed me up to the bridge where the captain was gone and a different man was at the wheel. The man had almost a perfect half circle taken out of the top of his left ear—it seemed to be a bite—and I wondered if he had gotten the bite in a hand-to-hand fight with Japs off a submarine that were trying to board his ship. I had heard about this on the radio once with Clara, but I didn't dare ask.

"The captain let us steer the ship," I said, and he smiled.

"He did, did he?"

"Yes. And told us about the compass, too."

"Well, we can't let the captain best us, can we?"

He let Jimmy steer and told Jimmy about the compass, which he called a rose, and we were getting so friendly and having such a good time that I came right out and asked him:

"Did some Jap off a submarine bite your ear when they were trying to board your ship?"

"Well, I'll be damned. You know, boy, that's *exactly* what happened. How did you know? Did somebody tell you?"

"I heard it on the radio. About the Japs from submarines boarding ships. And I thought that might be it." I shot a proud look at Jimmy but he was holding the wheel while he steered—or seemed to steer. He wasn't looking anywhere. Just staring at the floor, holding the wheel and staring down.

"Don't tell anybody, will you, boy?"

I shook my head. "Well, maybe my mother. But nobody else."

I decided Jimmy, who still hadn't said a word, wasn't having much fun so we left the bridge and moved down to the main deck again and went back to the stern to stand and watch the wake that went back like an arrow across the ocean.

Except there were sharks.

They were following the ship and you could tell they weren't dolphins because they were shaped differently, like arrows, and they didn't swim one over the other but just moved back and forth. It was hard to tell how many there were—over a dozen, maybe twenty—and I stared down at them in fascination and thought that some of them might be the same ones who hit the people from the plane, some of them maybe still had parts of people from the plane inside, I thought, and next to me I heard:

"Cocksuckers."

I turned and saw that Jimmy was staring down at the sharks. His eyes were on fire and he leaned forward so intently I thought he was going to climb the rail and jump down into them and start hitting them. But he held back and I took his arm and we left the stern.

We were four more days getting to Hawaii and that was the only word I heard him say, the only sound I heard him make, and he only said it once.

It was strange, but Jimmy and I became playmates even with his silence.

We explored the ship together.

Eleven

I learned from Mother that the plane had been coming home from Hawaii when it crashed. Now we were taking them all back to Hawaii and then they—the ones who survived the first try—would have to get on another plane and fly back to the States again.

I knew to say "the States." That's how everybody on the ship talked. They didn't say America or the United States—just the States. Jimmy had been in Hawaii for the whole war. His father was a pilot on a carrier and was due to get out of the service back in San Francisco. Jimmy and his mother were flying back to see him there. Well, just Jimmy now. Mother got this from the other people who had been on the plane, and she told me sitting in the cabin one night before we went to sleep.

It was the only time I ever saw her alone. The men still flocked around her during the day. She mostly helped Harding in the dispensary, but things settled down there somewhat by the second day after the crash and she would come on deck and walk for half an hour or just sit, and she was never alone. Twice I saw Harding with her, sitting on small canvas stools he'd found somewhere, the two of them on the bow looking up at the sun. He would talk quietly to her and she would nod or smile and shake her head, her hair flashing golden in the sun.

Now and then Harding would reach out and touch her, small touches on the cheek or to push hair back out of her face, and she didn't mind because she didn't stop him. She seemed to like it, as she seemed to like the attention of all the men.

It was not that she wanted them all to be like Uncle Casey because none of them touched her except Harding, and then I only saw him touch her cheek or her hair, not like Uncle Casey did. But she liked to be with them. To have the men around her.

Anytime she came on deck alone the soldiers would come to be close to her, to stand around her, to talk to her, and she smiled and nodded and put her hands to her hair and stood so her hip was jutting out a certain way that I had seen at the Cozy Corner in Chicago when she was dancing with the men from the war plant.

And the more men, the more soldiers, the better. She would laugh and joke with them and nod and if they stood too close so that some part of them started to touch her she would move away and laugh, looking down, and one night I asked her: "How come is it you always like men?"

She didn't say anything for a minute and then sighed. "Punkin, we said we weren't going to talk about things like this now that we're going to be with Daddy."

"We aren't with Daddy yet so I thought it was all right." We were in the cabin and it was after dark. I had climbed into the top bunk and leaned over so that I was looking down at her. "Men just come to you and come to you and you seem to like it . . ."

She laughed. "Well, sometimes. It's the way things are. Someday you'll want to be around girls."

"Not me. Not ever."

"Well, maybe it doesn't seem that way now but it will. There'll come a day when you'll think being around girls is the best thing in the world. And girls like that, too. It doesn't always mean anything. It's just nice, and kind of flattering."

After the second day I went back to the dispensary and found that most of my candy and comic books had been taken over by the people who were down there so I had none of those things left. But the cooks were men, too, and they had seen Mother in the galley and they gave me things. I could eat as much as I wanted and then they would let me take a cup of fruit cocktail back to the cabin with me and I sat and ate it in the top bunk while Mother talked some nights and the ship rumbled and moved through the ocean.

"Why is it you don't see the captain so much anymore?" I asked the night before we were due to arrive in Honolulu. Mother had told me that the captain had told her the ship originally had been scheduled to bypass the Hawaiian Islands but had to go there now to drop off the survivors of the plane crash. "He seemed nice and you were together that night in San Francisco . . ."

"That wasn't the same as this other thing with the men. He is a nice man, but he has to work on the ship and he was just being helpful so we could leave. We went out and danced and talked and he told me all about his family. He has four daughters back in Los Angeles . . ."

And I tried to keep it all straight in my mind, how the captain was different from Harding and how he might be different from Uncle Casey and how they were different from all the soldiers and how all of them were different from Father, but it was confusing and I went to sleep the night before Honolulu without understanding it, nor did I come to understand it later.

The ship did not go to a dock when we got to Honolulu. It stopped out in a bay and dropped anchor with a great rattling sound and a huge splash when the anchor hit the water. You could see the city and the buildings and the shore. I thought it looked very green and there were clouds over the islands and it seemed like I hadn't seen clouds for a long time. As soon as the anchor was down dozens of large canoes came around the ship and there were boys and girls yelling at us and making beckoning gestures with their hands.

"They want you to throw money over the side," Harding said. He was standing next to Mother, waiting for a boat that would come so they could transfer the survivors from the ship to the shore.

"How much money?"

"Oh, you know, pennies and nickels."

"Harding," I said—I never did learn his first name—"they're jumping right in the water after the money." Some of the soldiers were throwing pennies.

He nodded. "Sometimes that's all the money they get, what they can catch from the ships."

"But the sharks, Harding. Why don't the sharks get them?"

"I don't know, but they never do. Maybe it's because there isn't any blood. Some of the people on the plane were injured and maybe it was their blood in the water that set the sharks off."

I shivered and decided not to watch because I didn't believe that the sharks wouldn't come and I didn't want to see it. Thinking of the sharks made me think of Jimmy and I ran to find him to say good-bye. He was with the group of survivors waiting by a stairway that had been lowered down the side of the ship. I said good-bye to him, and he looked at me but didn't say anything.

A boat was coming from shore, a kind of large, square boat, and as I stood with Jimmy it came alongside and tied up to the platform at the bottom of the lowered stairway. Harding and Mother showed up at my back and Harding said:

"Let's go."

"Us, too?"

"Yes, we're going to help them."

Soldiers had to carry some of the survivors down, following

Harding's instructions, and Mother went along, helping them as she could. I followed Jimmy down into the boat.

It was all gray and there was a sailor at a steering wheel in the rear. He smiled at us and spat over the side. I saw a tattoo of a naked woman on his arm and she seemed to have nice tits so I whispered to Jimmy:

"Look at the tattoo on the sailor's arm. Nice tits, eh?"

He didn't say anything, but this time he looked at me and I thought he smiled.

When all the survivors were on board the boat the sailor nodded and another sailor untied the ropes. He gunned the engine and we moved away from the ship. Jimmy and I ran to the front of the boat, weaving through the stretchers on the bottom, and watched Honolulu.

"Over there," somebody said. "See? That's Pearl Harbor."

Of course I had heard of Pearl Harbor and I looked, but it didn't seem to be much. There were many navy ships there, you could see the tops of them, and I thought I saw a battleship, but I didn't know what they really looked like and it didn't matter because it was too far away to tell anything.

The boat went right up to a dock where there were gray-painted ambulances waiting and they made all the survivors, even the ones that weren't hurt, like Jimmy, get into the ambulances and that was the last we saw of them. Mother and Harding showed some papers to some men at the dock and we were released.

"Let's see if we can beat the rest of them from the boat and get rooms," Harding said. He waved at a car that turned out to be a taxi, even though it wasn't yellow. It was being driven by a huge, fat woman who smiled at us.

"Where to, boss?"

"The Royal . . ."

She gunned the engine and the cab jumped forward, slamming me into the seat between Harding and Mother. In a short time she pulled up in front of a hotel that had palm trees and plants in big pots all over the place. You could hardly see the building.

Harding led the way into the hotel. Inside the lobby it was cool and dark and quiet. The man at the desk nodded, said they had rooms, and Mother and Harding checked in while I looked at a man who had slanted eyes and glasses and was sitting in a chair reading the paper.

"Is that a Jap?" I asked Harding.

He shook his head and held his finger to his lips. "He's a Chinese man and you have to be careful of how you talk."

The man hadn't heard me, or at least didn't show any sign, and we went up a stairway—the elevator wasn't working—to where our rooms were. Harding had taken a room right next to ours, and he left us.

Mother opened the door and we went into the room. It had two beds and a window that looked out through the tops of palm trees on a beach to the ocean. Mother had brought a small bag from the ship and she dropped it on one of the beds and went to the window.

"Oh, look, Punkin, isn't it beautiful?"

And it was, too. There was a big mountain on the left side and the ocean out in front and the palm trees and the sun. Of course we'd seen the ocean before, but not with the trees and beach.

"Can we go to the beach?"

She nodded. "Harding said we would be here two nights while they do something to the ship. We're just supposed to relax. The captain is paying for everything because he said I helped so much with the people from the plane crash."

"Can I go to the beach now?" The sand looked so clean, and I thought maybe I could wade if I didn't go out deep enough for there to be sharks.

She nodded. "There are lifeguards. But you stay just in front of the hotel so they can see you . . ."

I was gone before she finished the sentence, still in what would turn out to be my almost constant uniform for the next two and a half years—too-large khaki shorts held up by an army belt with a brass buckle. Mother had tried to get me into regular clothes without success. The belt could easily go around me twice, but it never occurred to me to cut it off. Instead I just pulled it on through the buckle and let the brass end hang down and flop against my leg. I wore no shirt and no shoes and already, in just the week or so since I'd been let out of my cabin on the ship, I had burned and reburned and started to tan so that I was the color of the brown army shoes worn by the soldiers. My hair, normally a light blond, had already started to bleach white, as well as my eyebrows, and the top of my nose was sunburned, peeled, and reburned and would not tan so that I wore a small white bandage that Mother replaced daily.

Soldiers were coming through the lobby as I ran past and onto the beach. I could see the ship beyond the end of a temporary wharf made of pilings and interlocking metal stripping. It seemed small, and by squinting I could just make out the canoes still around it and another boat pulling away with more soldiers.

The beach sand was hot where the sun had free access, but my feet were already toughened by the deck of the ship and I trotted easily down to the water.

The lifeguard sat in an elevated chair. He looked very old—older than my uncles in northern Minnesota ever looked— and was bald with a white beard and a huge bare stomach. He seemed to be sound asleep.

Down from his chair and a few feet up the beach was a pile of junk, steel parts and aluminum folded in on itself, and I walked closer to it.

"It was a Jap bomber." The voice boomed, a hollow, carrying sound, and I turned to see that it was the lifeguard speaking. He still had his eyes closed, but he was smiling. All his teeth were gone. "From Pearl Harbor."

"But the war is over." I turned back to the wreckage, amazed that I was standing this close to something so malevolent, so evil, as an actual Jap plane. For years on the radio they were the yellow devils, the evil yellow devils, and their planes were always shot down with screams and curses by Terry and the Pirates or Buzz Armstrong. And here it was. I leaned closer and sure enough, there was Japanese writing on some tubes sticking out of what must have been the engine.

"The wreckage of war lasts longer than the war," he said. "Pearl Harbor is still not cleaned up. They will get to this when they get done with that." His mouth shut and he seemed to be asleep again.

I looked at the plane, but it was impossible to see it as a plane. It must have tumbled and crumpled as it rolled. There were no wings, at least nothing that looked like wings, and no tail, just smashed aluminum and the engine and on one piece of aluminum a small crescent of bright red.

That was it, I thought—the dreaded meatball. Or maybe it was Jap blood. I looked closer and decided it could have gone either way. I walked around the wreckage and tried to imagine how it had happened. He had attacked Pearl Harbor—I had seen pictures of that in newsreels so I knew about the attack and how it looked. I could see the pilot, his buck teeth smiling in an evil grin and his slanted eyes looking through the little goggles as he dropped his bombs on a ship in Pearl Harbor, and then he was laughing as he pulled up and escaped.

Or thought he had. But I could see the sailor on the machine gun, the one I'd seen in the newsreels, aiming up with grim determination on his face and the bullets hitting the plane and the Jap looking around in surprise at the flames, then the scream as he went down, crashing along the beach. Here it got a little fuzzy because I had visions of the plane crash I'd seen on the ocean, skipping and the splash of water but not getting crumpled this bad. So I visualized the Jap bomber hitting a tree as it came down, getting smashed by the tree, and I looked for a palm tree on the beach that had been shorn off. I couldn't find one but did see a tree with some marks on it and thought that might have been it and decided I'd better go and tell Mother about all of it.

As I trotted back to the hotel I saw that there were doors and windows on the beach side and that you could go up a stairway. I knew we were on the second floor and guessed at where the room was and ran up the stairway and down the long wooden balcony to where I thought our room was located.

The drapes were open and I saw Mother's bag on the bed, but the room was empty. I thought she must have gone down to the lobby for something so I tried the door, found it was locked, and turned to go back downstairs.

The turn took me past Harding's room. I had not looked in as I went by but did so now and saw that the drapes were closed.

Or nearly so. There was an open place next to the edge and a shaft of light went in from the sun and lighted that part of the room. I could see the bed and a table and a chair by the wall. Harding was sitting on the bed and Mother was standing by the table. As I watched he stood and went to her and put his hand beneath her chin and held her mouth up and kissed her on the mouth and she moved toward him, into him, then stepped back and shook her head. I couldn't hear what she said but I could see she didn't want to say no, didn't want to shake her head and Harding could see it too, see it the same way, and he moved to her and kissed her again and then they moved, moved away and out of sight, and I did not see any more. I thought of making a sound, tapping on the window, but I didn't. Instead I went back to the beach and sat next to the crumpled Jap bomber and was sitting there later when Mother came out of the hotel looking for me.

"Oh, here you are," she said. "I was beginning to worry about you." Her face was all flushed and she looked happy, and I didn't see how she could be happy with what she did with Harding, but

I didn't say anything. It seemed that if I talked about it it just made her feel bad—the way it did when I talked about Uncle Casey—and then it made things seem somehow tight between us, like when she was mad.

So I just sat, looking out across the beach at the ocean, and of course she knew something was wrong. She sat next to me on the beach and didn't say anything for a time. She had a small leather bag with her and she took a cigarette out of it and lit it with a Zippo lighter that had a picture of a plane on the side.

"Did you come up to the room a little while ago?" Her voice was light, but she had that tight sound and I tried to lie. Or sort of lie.

"Yes. I came up but you weren't there so I came back down here."

But of course you cannot lie to your mother, even when you think you can lie, because they know, they know, and so she knew I knew and had seen her with Harding, or at least thought it, and she hugged me.

"It's all grown-up stuff," she said. "You won't understand it for a long time and even then you might not like it all."

"I don't like it much now."

"I know, but there are some things grown-ups do that kids don't like and that's just the way it is, Punkin."

"Like drinking?" I asked. I didn't like it when she drank. She became all fuzzy and silly and sometimes seemed sloppy and it made the men around her worse.

"That, and being too serious, and . . ."

"Men. The messy thing with men and how they're always around you."

"Yes. That, too. Just like we talked about on the ship in the cabin that night."

I stared down at the sand for a minute or so. "I hope I grow up quick so I can understand and it won't make me so mad."

She hugged me again. "It will come soon enough—the growing up. Now, tell me what this is." And she pointed at the wreckage.

"It's a dead Jap plane from Pearl Harbor," I said. "I think it must have hit that tree and kind of rolled to get here. Look, you can see the Jap writing on it." And I showed her the Japanese writing on the tubes and she looked for a moment and then wasn't paying attention so well anymore and I looked up to see why. She was looking over me, over the wreckage, up at the hotel, and I turned to see that Harding had come out on the balcony and was standing in a bathing suit looking down at us. He was pale except for his face and hands and the swimming suit was a black wool that made him look even more pale.

He waved and Mother raised her hand and smiled at him, but I decided I didn't like him so much anymore and didn't wave and looked back at the engine.

Twelve

We were those two days in Hawaii, in the hotel on the beach. Mother as usual had men all around her but Harding most of all, and they spent a lot of time off alone. I tried to be with her as much as I could, but she would leave me on the beach and be gone for a time and then come back looking flushed and I decided if she wanted to be with old Harding more than me she could just do it.

I waded on the beach and went out until I could hardly see the lifeguard and it was still only up to my knees. I got stung by something and my arm was all swollen and I didn't know it until the lifeguard came down from his seat and wiped a kind of salve on it.

"It will go away. There are many things to sting you and you must be careful."

"I didn't see anything."

"Sometimes baby jellyfish are in clouds and they will sting you. They are so small you can't see them. Perhaps that is what happened."

"You talk funny."

"How is that?"

"Like a teacher in a movie or something. You make all the words sound long and full."

He smiled, showing his gums. "I think that might be a compliment."

I didn't know for certain what the word *compliment* meant so I didn't say anything. He helped me look for shells and by the end of the second day I had a good collection to take back to the ship in a small box with a picture of a beer bottle on the side.

The boat came for us in the evening and the ship pulled anchor just at dark while we stood on the deck and leaned on the rail and watched. Mother and I were alone. Harding had gone below to the dispensary and the soldiers were in a large room below the second deck, where they were shooting craps. I had seen them shoot craps before and didn't understand it but knew you could make a lot of money. I decided I would ask them to show me how to shoot a crap and get rich if I could. Mother went to the cabin—she instantly began to feel woozy when she came back on ship, having lost her sea legs after two days on shore—and I drifted toward the soldiers and the crap game.

It made no sense to me because of the way they threw the dice. They would lay money down and throw the dice and some of them would pick up the money and always, always there was a lot of swearing, which I thought was great.

I stood back, out on the edge. It was a room that had once been a galley for larger groups of people, when it was a true troopship and they had to feed hundreds of men instead of dozens. The tables were all gone, stacked and lashed back in a corner of the room, and the metal chairs were folded and gone as well. There was just one light—there were other bulbs but they were turned off or unscrewed—and it lighted a corner where the soldiers had spread a navy-blue blanket.

There must have been twenty or more of them, in pants and undershirts or open khaki shirts, and as soon as they saw me one of them said, "Here's the kid, her kid—hell, let him throw for me. I'll bet he's lucky. Anybody with a mother like that has to be lucky. Here kid, throw these little bastards for me—I'm losing my ass here. Come on, give the kid some room . . ."

He pulled me to the edge of the blanket and put the dice in my hand. I looked around at the faces, recognized some—Havermeyer was there and smiled at me. They had brought on crates and crates of Coca-Cola in Hawaii and he was drinking from a coke but it didn't look like Coca-Cola in the bottle. I smiled up at them.

"Right there, throw the dice." The blanket was curved up against the wall at the end and the soldier who had pulled at me pointed to the corner. "The dice have to bounce off that wall . . ."

"Come on, Jenkins, what the hell are you doing?"

"So what, you've got rules, asshole? Where does it say the kid can't throw for me? Come on, kid, throw."

I threw the dice, bouncing them off the wall, and they flicked and rolled and stopped.

"Seven," somebody said, and there was a bunch of swearing and Jenkins yelled and jumped forward to reach for the money—dollars around the edge of the blanket—and took them in. He handed me a dollar.

"Good going, kid. Now do it again."

I looked at the dollar. "Can I keep this?"

"You goddamn right you can keep it. It's yours and there's another one if you throw another pass for me."

I didn't know what he was talking about, but I could stand and throw the dice for a dollar a throw until my arms came off and I hoped Mother would go to sleep or stay in the bunk and that we would shoot a crap all night.

Men put money down again and I threw and this time I thought I should swear so I said, "Fuckerfart."

And threw the dice and didn't get a seven but I threw an

eleven and there was much more swearing and yelling and Jenkins raked in money and gave me another dollar and somebody handed me a coke and I felt like a man and thought maybe I would be a soldier when I grew up. I had wanted to be one before and then changed to a pilot, but seeing the wreck turned me away from that and I thought being a ship captain might be nice but he wasn't here drinking with the men and shooting a crap and making all that money so I was back to being a soldier, thinking my father would be proud of me if he could just see me now.

The ship rumbled and picked up speed and we were under way, but I hardly noticed it. I played dice with the soldiers until my arm felt numb. I didn't throw sevens or elevens all the time, but when I didn't I did something called making the point and I seemed to either get a seven or eleven or make my point almost all the time. And when Jenkins finally lost—or rather I lost for him—another soldier picked me up and each time I won for him or for the next one or the next one they gave me a dollar and I kept stuffing them into the pockets of my shorts.

When the game finally broke up because two soldiers got mad about something—I think it was a woman back in Honolulu because one of them accused the other of stealing his time with her—and started to fight, my shorts were full of wadded dollar bills and I had a date for the next night to come and shoot a crap again.

I couldn't tell what time it was, but I think it was the middle of the night when I got back to the cabin. Mother was sound asleep when I came in. She had a bucket by the bed and it had stuff in it from her throwing up. I dumped it in the toilet and put the bucket back and climbed into the top bunk and went to sleep with pictures of rolling dice and money and men swearing and drinking and laughing and then fighting all mixed in my mind.

Thirteen

Shipboard life changed for me after Honolulu. Mother was sick for three days, and weak for another day after that. She came out on deck but sat on a canvas chair in the sun and looked out across the blue. With all the survivors gone from the boat Harding had time on his hands and he spent it all with Mother.

He brought her soup, wiped her forehead, sat next to her on the deck and talked and read to her out of books he had that I didn't understand. Sometimes I would come into the cabin and find him sitting on the bed with her with his hand on her forehead or her cheek and Mother would look at me and smile. I never caught him doing anything else with her, but I think they did something because there is a smell after they do it that I used to smell when Uncle Casey did it and I smelled it sometimes in the cabin. It was a musty smell mixed with sweat and skin and something else and I didn't like it.

With Harding always with her, and with Mother sick for those days, and without Jimmy following me, I was wildly free. I went into all the parts of the ship that I might have missed before, including the engine room, where I thought I could have happily lived for the rest of my life.

Huge gears and shafts and rods and all of it working in heat and great noise and the smell of oil and grease—it was the heart, the guts, the brains of the ship and I felt that it was almost alive. There were men there, stripped to the waist and indescribably, wonderfully dirty. The chief engineer—he never told me his name and it wouldn't have mattered anyway because I don't think I would have been able to hear it—ruffled my hair with a greasy hand and handed me a cup of thick, black coffee stirred sticky sweet with heaping spoonfuls of sugar. He showed me dials and switches and springs and oil valves, slapping each with a filthy hand, laughing and joking with the other men, while I drank the coffee. It was hot but I couldn't make myself look bad in front of them and got it all down and it kept me awake until four the following morning. The engineer showed me all the nooks and crannies and I went back three times and sat in the corner of the engine room and just watched the men work. I probably could have spent the rest of the voyage down there except that I began to miss the sun and the blue sky and sea after having spent so much time in a windowless room during the first part of the trip.

I played craps again and again and one night watched the men while they played poker. It was in the same room and they had the same blanket on the floor and they were sitting on pillows they'd brought from their bunks. They played five-card stud and seven-card stud and draw poker, but I liked the stud games the best because the name sounded good to me.

"Stud," the dealer would say. "Seven-card. Ante a buck." And each time a card came down he would talk about the card and say things like "Eighter from Decatur," and "Whores and fours," or "Bullets and ducks."

And none of it made any sense to me, but I loved the way the dealer said the names and the money, great piles of money. It was just fun to see all the money. I didn't get any from poker like I did when they played craps, but it didn't matter because I had lots of money in the cabin saved in the small canvas bag I had for my clothes. Mother had seen the money and asked me about it with fire in her eye, but I explained how I got it and she just told me not to do it anymore, but she didn't say it strong like she meant it, and she didn't tell me to take the money back.

Sometimes during the poker games the men would send me for cokes that they kept in a big cooler in their sleeping area. They would usually give me a quarter for running for the coke plus I got half the soda because they really didn't want all of it. They would pour out half, or let me drink it, then add whiskey from a bottle with four roses on it or oily-smelling rum from a bottle with a black man with a big mouth on the label until the coke bottle looked full again.

It was necessary to go down a long passageway through the sailor's quarters to get to the room where the soldiers slept and kept their Coca-Cola. The sailors had their own cabins, with two men to a cabin and doors that opened onto the passageway. On one of the runs I went past a cabin with a man sitting on a chair and when I came back past the room the man had his pants down and was playing with himself. He smiled at me and beckoned but didn't say anything or move toward me and I ran on past and took the cokes to the game. But it had startled me and must have shown on my face.

Havermeyer was playing and had won lots of money. He seemed to win all the time but nobody got mad at him because he always joked about it and he was so big I don't think anybody dared.

He was dealing and he looked up as I came in with the cokes and said, "What's the matter, kid? You look like you swallowed a possum."

Without thinking I said, "One of the sailors was playing with himself and waved to me."

I could not have stopped the game faster had I dumped a bucket of water on the blanket.

There was immediate, stunned silence. Every man, not just the players but some who were watching or waiting for an opening so they could play—every single one of them looked at me.

"Are you sure, kid?" Havermeyer's voice was flat, even. "Are you really sure?"

I was, but it didn't matter. The soldiers were up and heading for the passageway to the sailors' quarters before I could answer the question. They even left the cards and money on the blanket, and I ran with them.

I hadn't meant them to do anything and as they started down the passageway one of them took my arm and pulled me to the front. "Show us—show us which one."

It all felt bad, but I was afraid that if I didn't show them they would just go after any sailor and might get the wrong one. I didn't know for sure what they were going to do, but I knew it wasn't going to be nice for the sailor because they were swearing and saying things like: "Fucking fairy" and "dirty cocksucker" and other things mixed with swearing so when we came to the sailor's cabin I pointed to it. The door was closed but two of the soldiers slammed it open and dragged me inside.

The sailor was lying on his bunk with a magazine. He had his pants and an undershirt on, but I was pretty sure it was the same one.

"What the hell?" The sailor tried to stand, but a soldier pushed him back on the bunk. He sat leaning forward. He was thin and had blond hair and thin lips and huge blue eyes. His lower lip was trembling and his eyes were full of fear.

"Is this the one?" Havermeyer asked.

I hesitated.

"Come on, kid—tell me the truth."

"That's him. He had a chair by the door and he was sitting in it and playing with his peter and when he saw me he waved for me to come in." It all came out in a rush.

One of the men grabbed the sailor by the hair—it was long and had oil in it—and dragged him to a standing position.

"Cut his fucking balls off!" somebody yelled, and somebody else said, "Yeah, give me a knife. Cut the fucking fairy's balls off."

I thought they were going to do it, but Havermeyer said, "No, he might bleed out if we do that. Give him a blanket party."

Which didn't sound too bad and I thought maybe everything would turn out all right.

Then one of the soldiers grabbed the blanket off the bunk and threw it over the sailor until it covered him and he couldn't see. And then all the soldiers took turns and they beat him and beat him through the blanket.

When he couldn't stand anymore and had peed and messed his pants, which I could smell, they dropped him but didn't stop beating him.

"Please don't," I said, but they didn't hear me and probably wouldn't have stopped if they had.

"In the body," Havermeyer said. "No more in the head—you'll kill the son of a bitch. Hit him in the body."

They kicked him and leaned down to hit him and one of them hit him again and again with the chair until the blanket was soaked in blood, a matted ugly mess of soaked blood stinking of urine and mess and finally, finally they stopped, and I thought of Mother and the drunk.

All this time Havermeyer held me and when the smell got bad and the blood got bad and the sound of them beating him got bad I couldn't help myself and threw up. But he still didn't let me go until at last they were done with him.

Then they filed out—it all hadn't taken more than four or five minutes—and Havermeyer let go of my hand. I wanted to run but I stood there, looking down at the blanket, listening to the small sounds the sailor made, looking at the blood coming out, and I wanted the trip to be over, all of it.

I wanted everything to go backward. The plane to unwreck and Mother not to be with men anymore and the sailor to be back on the chair playing with his peter and everything, everything, to be like it was with the war still going on and me sitting in the apartment in Chicago with Clara, listening to the radio, and I closed my eyes and wished hard, as hard as I could, but when I opened them I saw that it wouldn't.

Nothing would go backward.

I left the sailor and went up to our cabin. Mother was gone so I sat on my bunk and wondered about the sailor, hoping he wouldn't die, and wishing I wasn't wrong so much of the time.

Fourteen

I thought they had killed the sailor. After the plane crash it seemed that people could die easily even if they didn't seem to have all that much wrong with them. They would sit and be quiet and almost smile and they would look at you and die, and I thought the soldiers had killed the sailor because he was all blood and making funny sounds.

I didn't play poker or shoot a crap for a couple of days, worrying that I had caused them to kill a man who was just playing with his peter and in my memory I couldn't even be sure he had beckoned to me or maybe he was just waving.

I stayed around Mother and colored. Some of the men had given me coloring books when I was sick—I found later the cook had a pile of them (he did them himself) and made good money for a while selling them to soldiers who wanted to impress Mother—and I sat and colored for almost two whole days. I did all of a Porky Pig and a Donald Duck book, and even used black crayon to go around the lines after the colors were in and kept them neat, and did part of a Captain Marvel sitting in the cabin.

I didn't like Captain Marvel because the lines were already too dark and it didn't help to make them black.

After the first day Mother put her hand on my forehead.

"Are you sick?"

"No. I just want to color . . . ."

"You don't feel hot, but you're acting sick." Her voice had that suspicious edge to it, the way it sounded when I was small and she used to ask me if I had gone in my pants.

By the next afternoon when I sat and colored and didn't run and play she shook her head. "Well, this is too strange. Come on, let's have Harding take a look at you."

I didn't like Harding any longer and didn't want to see him, but I didn't say anything and she walked me down to the dispensary where Harding was and on the way we went past my old cabin and there was the sailor.

He looked all lumpy and black and blue and his eyes were closed, but he was sitting up in the bed and he was alive.

Mother saw me look at him as we went by. "Isn't that awful? Some soldiers beat him up. The captain is trying to find out about it, but nobody will say anything. Even Harding doesn't know why they did it."

Harding of course found nothing wrong with me, though he prodded and pushed and stuck a thermometer in my mouth that tasted of alcohol and in a short time they let me go.

Relieved of guilt because the sailor wasn't dead, I put the coloring books away and once more used the ship for a playground.

I found out where we were going next. I had always thought we were just going to the Philippine Islands, which I did not know about except that Mother had shown me pictures in a magazine. The pictures were in *Life* and were black and white and showed some jungle and a bunch of buildings blown up, and I thought that was probably all there was there, blown-up buildings and jungles on a small island. Or maybe two islands. And I thought that was where we were going.

But I heard the soldiers say the ship was going next to Okinawa. I knew it was Japanese because I heard the soldiers talking about it—most of them were going to be stationed there in what they called the occupation forces. They also said a lot about the Japanese women, some of which I understood and some of which I didn't but which sounded interesting.

I was terribly excited and a little afraid about going to Okinawa because of the Japanese, and for almost two days I went to the bow of the ship often to watch the horizon, thinking that we would see it momentarily. One of the soldiers finally told me that we would be at least another week getting there, and I returned to my normal schedule of play.

Finally one night I was sitting in the cabin with Mother and she said: "Tomorrow we're supposed to get to Okinawa. We stay there just one night while the soldiers get off. All these soldiers are going there to help rebuild it, isn't that nice?"

"But they're Japs, aren't they?"

Mother nodded.

"Why are we helping them?"

She smiled. "It's too complicated to understand."

"Can we go on the shore?"

"Yes. The captain said we could spend some time in the afternoon after we arrive. But we have to be back by dark."

I went to sleep that night with visions of slanty-eyed bucktoothed devils and I wished I had a gun because you could never trust a Jap . . .

Fifteen

 In Okinawa the ship came into a dock, a large wharf with tin shacks scattered around it.

The captain had announced the day before that we would be arriving just at dawn and I was awake before Mother to see it. The problem was that it had been getting progressively colder through the day and when I stepped quietly out of the cabin to watch the ship as it approached the land I was surprised to see that it was snowing.

I was still in shorts and tennis shoes, though I had thrown a T-shirt on, and I ran back in to awaken Mother.

"It's snowing," I said.

"What?" It was still dark outside, but I had turned on the cabin overhead light that slashed the room with flat white.

"Snow!" I ran to the door and opened it but nothing showed. "It's snowing outside . . ."

She put on a robe and came to the door and looked out across the water. "So it is."

"I didn't think it did—snow on the ocean. Where does it go?"

"It just melts when it hits the water. Why don't you be a good boy and find Mommy a cup of black coffee."

I went to the galley and brought her back two cups—I knew one wouldn't be enough—and then I found a sweatshirt and went out to play in the snow.

I thought it might accumulate on the deck, but it really wasn't that cold and the snow melted as soon as it hit the steel.

It was getting light, gray and even, as if the light came from all around, and I could see that we were in a harbor working our way to the wharf. There were tugboats in the front and back pushing sideways to bring the ship in.

As early as it was, there were people everywhere. They were jammed in crowds waiting for the ship to come into the dock, and as we were pushed into place by the tugs, nudging us front and back, and the sailors yelled and cursed while they tied the ropes to hold the ship in, I was amazed to see that every single person on the dock was Japanese.

I ran back into the cabin. "Don't come out."

"What?" Mother had dressed in slacks and a sweater and was doing her makeup. "What's the matter with you?"

"Japs. There's thousands of them. I think they're going to attack the ship. Stay in here and we'll hide."

Mother smiled. "That's over, all over. You don't have to worry now."

"But they're all over the place. You don't know. Even in pictures in the magazine I never saw so many Japs."

She went to the door and opened it and looked out and down on the dock. It was much brighter now and she could see well.

"They're all women," she said. "And children. They're here to beg—they won't hurt you." She came back into the cabin to finish her makeup, but she wasn't smiling any longer. Her eyes looked sad and I thought she was going to cry. "All the women and all the children—there are no men left. They were all killed—goddamn them."

I went back outside tentatively and leaned on the rail looking down, ready to run back into the cabin if necessary. Mother had been right. In all the press of people I didn't see more than three or four men and they were very old. All the rest were children and women but they didn't look like beggars.

In Hawaii the children and people in the canoes were dressed in odds and ends, almost rags. The people here looked clean and neat and were very quiet. Their clothes were colorful, silk cloaks and kimonos with embroidered flowers and patterns on them. Bright reds and yellows and everything, even on the children, everything neatly in place. Every hair. Little white edges of collars shown at the top of the kimonos. Crisp. Clean.

I couldn't think of them as the buck-toothed slanty-eyed devils. I tried. I had just had four years of constant bombardment with news about how evil they were, how horrible, and I tried to hate them. But I couldn't.

They were packed on the dock and as the ship finally was warped into position the children raised their hands.

There was none of the boisterous, raucous noise there had been in Hawaii. The children just quietly raised their hands and the women looked down.

There were no soldiers on deck. They did not get up early. But Mother came out then and stood there with me, looking down at them, standing in the dawn light, the children holding their hands up in the faint snow with the colors of the silk cloaks splashing red and yellow and deep shining black on the dock and the sailors yelling and swearing but no other sound. Just the ship's engines rumbling and the sailors and the quiet children and women and the falling, gentle snow.

"Oh Jesus God," Mother said. "Oh Jesus God." I looked up and she was crying, her mascara streaking down her cheeks, and I thought maybe she was swearing about them, about something, but then I decided it was a prayer. "What have we done? Oh Jesus God, what have we done?"

She went back into the cabin again, but I stood and watched all the time, all the while they tied the ship and all that time the children stood with their hands up while their mothers looked at the ground and I couldn't think of them as buck-toothed slanty-eyed devils and did not think I ever would again.

Sixteen

Mother decided to not go ashore and I think she would have stuck to it. But the soldiers all left the ship and when they had gone ashore—I stood by the gangplank and watched them, with their duffel bags on their shoulders, and many of them waved to me—much of the crowd of women and children had melted away.

Harding came to the cabin and talked to Mother and finally she agreed to go. After she fixed her makeup she took my hand and we went down the gangplank.

There were still some people there, women in bright kimonos and children. The women kept their faces down, but the children came forward and smiled shyly at us and held out their hands.

"Chewing gum?" they said, except that it came out *choon-gung*. "Chewing gum?"

Mother had a huge brown leather purse and she had things in it. Before I knew what was happening she was handing out candy—I later found it was my candy—and cans of milk from the galley.

As soon as she started to reach in her purse the children came forward, more and more, and still more came from the metal shacks along the wharf until we were stopped in a press of them and Mother had handed out all she had brought. And through it all they never made a sound, not a whisper. I was frightened and had moved closer to Mother and held tightly to her hand. They were, children or not, all Japs and full of treachery and I couldn't believe that Mother wasn't worried.

"No more," she said. "I'm sorry. I'm so sorry, but there isn't any more . . ."

They politely backed away, cleared an aisle, and we walked up from the dock. I looked back and the children took what they had received from Mother—it might be a can of condensed milk or a small candy bar—and gently handed it to their mothers and not once did the mothers look up or say anything. As soon as we were moving they all followed us.

I'm not sure what I expected on Okinawa. I had seen news-reels of fighting against the Japanese, but I could see no signs of war here. There were many, many shacks by the docks, made of corrugated roofing and metal matting with holes in it that was also on the ground to walk on as we moved away from the ship.

We did not go far. The warm air on the Pacific had made us unaccustomed to cold and it was still lightly snowing and I was wearing shorts with a sweatshirt. My legs were soon close to blue and Mother, even in her slacks, was shivering.

"I don't know, Punkin . . ." She stopped and I stopped next to her. "Maybe this wasn't such a good idea."

Other than very old men with white or gray beards there were no men in sight. But there were still many women and some children who followed us, stopping well back when we stopped, coming again as we walked.

The shacks, the tin and wood shacks, did not seem run down. In a strange way they were neat and clean and I saw that some of them were small cafés with raised front openings and had bowls of cold rice with other things in them and one had steam coming from it and the steam made my mouth water.

In that one an old woman—she might have been forty but that seemed ancient to me—smiled at us, and Mother walked to the front of her shack.

She said something in Japanese that we could, of course, not understand but held out a small porcelain cup and Mother nodded and took it. There was a crudely lettered sign that I could not read except that it said a word followed by 5¢.

"Why, it's tea, Punkin," Mother said. "It's some wonderfully smelling tea. Here, take a sip."

I thought it might be poisoned, but it smelled so good and seemed so warm and the weather was so cold that I took a sip from it. It tasted green and had a tang to it, and Mother paid the woman a quarter and we drank two more, standing by the shack with children out in a circle watching us and their mothers behind them.

The woman wore a brightly colored kimono with flowers down each side of the front and I leaned forward to see below the level of the window, to see if the flowers went all the way to the ground.

She smiled and reached out a hand and touched my hair and said something to Mother that meant nothing to me, except the look in her eyes suddenly became sad and one tear left her eye and slid down her right cheek while she was touching my hair, smiling at me. I looked at Mother and she was crying as well, which didn't make any sense except that I think the woman maybe had children and they were gone and that made her sad and Mother felt it, felt the sadness.

It was embarrassing and I moved back closer to Mother and the woman let her hand drop and Mother set her teacup down. I held mine for a moment, feeling the last of the heat from the porcelain, then put it on the counter. It had a green fish with flowers that wrapped around the side and the fish seemed to be eating its own tail. I stared at it for a moment and the woman took it from the counter and handed it to me.

"She wants you to have it, Punkin." Mother dug in her purse and brought out a dollar, but the woman would not take it. She kept pushing the teacup into my hand but waved the dollar away and finally Mother put it back in her purse.

"Thank her, Punkin."

"Thank you," I said and the woman nodded and bowed and I bowed back and we left the front of her shack.

"Wasn't that sweet, Punkin?" Mother said. "To give you that cup? They don't have anything—nothing at all left. And she gave you that cup. And it's beautiful, isn't it?"

I walked along holding the cup looking at the fish and flowers on the side and all things, all my thinking, was upside down. Except for their clothing and their narrower eyes and thick black hair, the children standing quietly by the wharf with their hands in the air were my size, many of them, and I wondered how it would be if Mother had to stand and look at the ground and I stood by a ship when soldiers came down the gangplank and held my hand in the air for cans of milk or candy bars or chewing gum.

We did not walk long. There were more shacks—Mother called them shops—and there were many things that smelled good, but Mother would not let me eat them. She pulled me past the shops that had the food smells coming from them and one place that had two women standing out in front in kimonos, where two soldiers were talking to them and touching them the way some men touched Mother.

When the shacks ended, abruptly, at the end of the docks there was very little left, a dirt road that vanished in the snow that was now mixing with rain. I heard some of the soldiers say that there was a city not too far away, but you could not see it from the dock and Mother and I turned and walked back to the ship through the group of quiet children and mothers who had been following us.

They turned and continued to follow us. All the way back down past the row of shacks and to the gangplank they followed us in silence and watched as we walked back up to the deck of the ship.

Mother took me to the cabin and wrapped me in a blanket where I sat shivering.

"Wait here, Punkin." She left and came back in a few minutes with some hot chocolate. It tasted different from the hot chocolate Harding had given me—sweeter.

"Where did you get the hot chocolate?"

"It's one of your Hershey bars and a can of milk," she said. "Good, isn't it?"

It warmed me inside and out and I thought of going back out again and seeing if the children and women were still there, but Mother was ahead of me.

"I've talked to the galley again," she said. "They're going to go through all their stores and anything that's extra we can give to the people on the dock . . ."

She rushed out of the cabin once more and came back in a few minutes with Harding. Both of them were loaded down with boxes, and they went back to the galley several more times.

"Your mother is a one-woman Red Cross," Harding said.

When she had stripped the galley of everything she could get, the three of us carried the boxes down the gangplank to the bottom and handed the items out one at a time.

There was still no sound. Children went silently back and forth carrying cans and boxes—it was mostly cans of lima beans, which the sailors and soldiers didn't like, and small boxes of crackers that even I couldn't eat. They were packed in cardboard and wax paper and were round, brittle, and tough and tasted like wood. There were also cans of pork and beans, some more cans of milk, and several boxes of cans that were very light, which Mother told me held dehydrated potatoes.

When we were done handing the food out we turned to go

back on the ship, but one of the women came forward. She looked up and straight into Mother's eyes and didn't say anything but took her kimono off and put it around Mother's shoulders.

The woman was very tiny and the kimono was clearly too small, but it was beautiful, all silky with embroidered flowers and a long-legged bird down the back. Mother took it off and tried to put it back on the woman, who had been wearing a white cotton wrap-around blouse beneath it. But the woman shook her head and pushed it back on Mother's shoulders and turned and ran away before Mother could make her take it back.

Mother watched her go, watched the rest of them turn and go, and then we made our way back up the gangplank. We were near the top when a voice stopped us:

"What's this I hear about you giving away food from my ship?"

Mother and Harding stopped and I bumped into them. We looked up to see the captain standing at the top of the gangplank.

"They don't have anything . . . ," Mother started to say. She was half smiling because she thought the captain was maybe joking, but I saw his eyes and knew he wasn't.

"That doesn't matter. I will be the one who decides what is given away on this ship." I saw Mother's back stiffen and could tell from the way her arms straightened that she was angry as well. But her voice was still even and soft.

"I just assumed you wouldn't mind," she said. "So I asked the cooks for food that was extra." She took a breath and made her voice sound sweet. "Would you like me to catch them and take it back?"

There was silence for a moment. Harding coughed and the captain looked at him. "You should know better."

"Aye, aye, sir."

"I was the one who did it," Mother said. "Not him. He just helped me carry it."

"He should know better."

"Than to give food to starving children?"

The captain stared at her for a long time, then turned and walked off toward the bridge.

"He was really pissed," Harding said.

"What's the difference?" Mother asked. "It's a bunch of crap nobody wants to eat, isn't it?"

Harding's face took on a strange twist, a half smile and half smirk or grimace. The snow was turning to rain and we were still standing out on the deck and the water ran down his forehead into his eyes. "The captain sells that stuff."

"What?"

"It's common in merchant marine. Sometimes the cooks do it, sometimes the captains. They sell the extra food nobody wants and pocket the money. You talked the cooks out of it, but it's really the captain's food and that's why he's mad."

"Well, fuck him."

It startled me to hear her say it. I had heard her swear many times and even use that word, but there was an edge to it now, a cutting part, and it seemed to crackle and I felt that if the captain had argued with her or tried to take the food back she would have knocked him down and kicked him in the temple the way she did the drunk.

But the captain did not come back. Harding went to the dispensary to change clothes and Mother and I went to our cabin, where she dressed me in warm clothes and we had some more hot chocolate and coffee and I spent the rest of the day coloring and wishing we could leave Okinawa.

Mother brought sandwiches up from the galley for dinner and we ate in the cabin and went to bed early and sometime in the night I heard the engines thrum louder.

I awakened to see Mother standing at the open door of the cabin. She was wearing her housecoat, but she was holding the silk kimono the woman had given her. She held it against her cheek, rubbing it there, looking out the door, and I could feel the ship moving as the tugs pushed her away from the dock, and in the light from the wharves, the pale light through the soft rain and snow that was still falling, I could see that Mother's eyes were damp.

"It's all right," I said, rubbing my eyes. "Pretty soon we'll see Daddy and it will be all right."

She turned. "For us, Punkin, yes it will. It will be all right. But not for them. Not ever again for them."

She closed the cabin door and came to me and took me from the top bunk. And we sat together on the bottom one and she sang a song in Norwegian that she said she learned from her mother, my grandmother, and I went to sleep leaning against her side with the silk kimono against my face, silky and smooth and smelling of lavender.

Seventeen

In a short time—a day and a night—we were back in warm weather and I was back to shorts with an old army belt holding them up.

The ship had changed.

With all the soldiers gone it seemed terribly empty and because of Mother's run-in with the captain I was not so welcome as I had been on the bridge if he was there. The sailors loved Mother—more so after they learned what she had done—and treated me better than before, if possible, but not when the captain was around.

I haunted the old places now, where I had learned to shoot craps and play poker, and I kept seeing the sailor the soldiers had beaten up, but he didn't bother me again. In fact once in the galley I was waiting in line with my tray to get food and I looked up and he was standing right next to me. When he saw me look at him he quickly looked away and let me move ahead of him a ways in the line.

One morning I went out on deck and the sea all around the ship was covered with flying fish. I had seen them many times, but not like this—there were clouds of them. I heard yelling and saw they had lowered a stairway down the side of the ship; two of the cooks were down at the bottom with a long-handled net, scooping them up and dropping them in a big tub.

I wanted to go down on the stairway, but Harding came on deck and saw me just then and shook his head. "Wait until they come up."

When they had nearly filled the tub they brought it back on deck to the stern and cleaned the fish, dropping the guts on the deck and then hosing them off to the waiting sharks.

I watched the sharks for a little while, frothing back and forth in the blood and guts that sprayed off the stern, and I remembered the wreck and Jimmy. It seemed to have happened years ago. Now I could look at the sharks and except for shivering a little they didn't bother me at all. I went back to watching the men clean the fish.

The flying fish were pretty. The long fin-wings seemed to glow when they caught the light and they let me hold them up and look at them, but I didn't want to help clean them though I did touch the guts once, poking at a bladder-looking thing with my finger and jumping when one of the cooks pushed my shoulder and said, "Gotcha."

That night the cooks deep-fried the fish with some kind of batter on them, just dipping each fish and dropping them in the bubbling, hot fat. Everybody came to the galley, even the captain and the sailor who had been beaten, and there was a party with everybody eating fish and drinking beer out of olive-drab cans with black letters on the side.

I thought the fish tasted good and ate until I was so full I couldn't hold any more. Mother ate a bite from one and then stopped—she said they were too oily—but she drank a beer and then another beer.

There were sailors around her, as there had been soldiers when they were on the ship, and as soon as she emptied a beer one of them would use a pointed opener to make holes in another one and hand it to her and soon she was drunk.

I didn't like it when she became drunk and so I moved off to the side of the galley. The cooks had set up a phonograph and the sailors were asking Mother to dance. It seemed that she danced with every man there, and most of them twice, the sailors pushing at each other to get in line and be next and many of them touch-ing her, touching her wrong, but she was so drunk and laughing and her hair flying around and she didn't notice or maybe didn't care.

Harding sat at a table drinking beer. Just one beer he had. He would raise the brown can and take a small sip and set it back on the table and watch Mother dance, watch her until I thought his eyes would burn right through her, but she didn't stop.

Finally he stood and walked across the galley. She was danc-ing close with a sailor from the engine room, not even caring that he was still dirty from work, and Harding tapped him on the shoulder and the man turned to him and said, "Fuck off, doc, it's my turn."

Harding hit him on the side of the head, but Harding had thin arms and narrow shoulders and not as much weight as the man from the engine room. The sailor turned and brought his knee up between Harding's legs and Harding doubled over and fell back to the tables at the side of the room.

"What are you doing?" Mother asked. But her voice was slurred and thick and she was having trouble staying on her feet.

"We're dancing and he was bothering us. Now come on, let's dance." And the sailor took her back again, held her close, too close and too tightly, and started whirling her around the floor. It wasn't dancing. Even I could see that. He was just rubbing against her and moving faster and faster and spinning her around and around, laughing low in his throat, and I wondered if I could go out and get him to stop, but I didn't have to.

"That's enough . . ."

The captain was standing at the end of the room by the door. He had been drinking beer and I think he had been about to leave when it all started.

"I said that's enough, Kowalski. Let her be."

The sailor from the engine room stopped, but he didn't let Mother go and for a moment I thought he was going to disobey the captain and I wondered if the captain would have him shot because I had seen in a movie where if a sailor disobeyed him a captain could have him shot.

But then he let her go, turned, and walked away.

"Stop the music," the captain told the cooks. "That's enough for tonight."

There was a squeak as one of the cooks lifted the arm of the phonograph off the record and the music stopped. Mother stood in the middle of the floor, looking down, then up and around. On top of the drinking I think she was dizzy from Kowalski whipping her around and around. She had a bewildered look on her face.

"Get her," I heard and turned to see Harding. He was leaning against the table, holding himself, doubled over. "Go get her and take her back to the cabin."

I moved from the corner of the galley and took Mother's hand and led her from the room. It was quiet, so quiet you could hear the men breathing and Mother's shoes shuffling as I led her from the galley out into the passageway and up a stairway and out to the deck and into our cabin.

"Oh, Punkin, I'm so sick . . ."

I helped her to her bed and she fell on it and turned sideways and vomited on the floor where the seasick bucket had been. I brought two olive-drab towels from the toilet cubicle and dropped them on the mess and then brought the bucket and put it next to her bed in case she needed it again.

It wasn't late, but I was tired so I crawled into my bunk and tried to sleep. But it didn't come and I lay for a long time thinking of the night, the dancing, and the way Mother became when she drank, and I thought that I would never drink.

Then I wished Harding had hit the sailor from the engine room in the nuts before he hit Harding and when he was down I could come and kick him, but that didn't last long and, finally, I went to sleep.

Eighteen

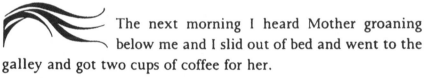The next morning I heard Mother groaning below me and I slid out of bed and went to the galley and got two cups of coffee for her.

"Oh, Jesus God, what did I do?" she said when I gave her the coffee.

"You drank army beer out of brown cans and then danced with every sailor and then one sailor danced funny with you and Harding tried to stop him and he kicked Harding in the nuts . . ."

"Thank you, Punkin—I remember. I should have said why did I do it, not what did I do."

She sat up on the bunk and saw the bucket and the two towels. "Did you clean it up?"

I nodded. "Sort of. I can't touch it because it makes me sick, but I put the towels in it and kind of folded them over it."

"I'm sorry, Punkin."

I didn't say anything.

"Did . . . anybody come back to the cabin with us?"

"No. I brought you up here and put you to bed and then you got sick and . . ."

She held up her hand and took a sip of coffee.

"There's another cup over on the table," I said.

She nodded. "You take good care of your mother, don't you?"

I shrugged. "I wish you didn't do that. Drink and dance and be that way with men."

"We've talked about that, remember? When you're older you'll understand."

I was going to say more about how I didn't want to understand but just didn't want her to do it and that Father wouldn't like it, but there was a pounding on the door.

I opened it to see Harding.

"Quick! Come on outside—the *Missouri* is passing us."

I turned to Mother and she waved. "Go ahead—I'll be along in a bit."

I ran outside and stopped dead.

I don't know what I expected—maybe to see a ship way off in the distance, or the smoke from the stacks.

Instead I saw a great, gray wall. It was such a surprise that it frightened me and I jumped back.

"Come on," Harding said. "It's all right. Look at her—it's the first time I've seen her."

I moved back to the outside deck and stood, looking up and my thoughts were so stunned, so shocked that I just took Harding's hand and opened my mouth and stared.

All this time, all that I knew of the war had either been in black-and-white newspaper pictures or magazines or black-and-white newsreels or two films that Mother and Uncle Casey had taken me to see about the war.

Everything had been in black and white and had been on a very small scale. I had no idea, really, of the enormity of the war—of how raw, how *big* it was. There had always been small pictures of small boats and small airplanes all in controllable amounts. And there was no color. Except for advertising in magazines and now and then a picture of a pretty girl, everything of or about the war was in different tones of gray.

And here it was all at once—all blown apart at once.

The sea was the same rich blue, the sky to match, and this . . . this *huge* wall of gray, battleship gray, was moving past us, roaring past us, thundering past us with a great froth of white water at the bow and guns and more guns and men running back and forth in blue dungarees and *still* more guns. It seemed there were gun barrels sticking out of every nook and cranny, bristling like hairs. And her huge cannon lay out flat in front and back and just those, just the cannons, seemed bigger than our whole ship.

I had to look up to see her, up from our deck. Up and up and up. She was moving three, four times as fast as we were and was nearly alongside before Harding told us and now she was moving away in front, away and away, and in just moments it seemed she was far enough in front of us to be back to newsreel size.

"Jesus Christ," I said.

I felt pressure against my back and turned to see Mother standing against me. She had come out without my knowing. But she didn't say anything about my swearing. Instead she was holding a hand to her mouth, the tips of her fingers to her lower lip, and her eyes were wide and staring.

"How in God's name did they expect to beat us?" she said. "How can anybody expect to beat that?"

Harding nodded. "Right. Except the Japs had a bigger one. The biggest one ever made. We sank the son of a bitch."

And he said it with pride even though he was in the merchant marine and not the real navy and in a strange way I felt the same pride and I think Mother did, too.

"It was all gray," I said. "But not like in the pictures. Kind of a gray with blue in it and so . . . so clean. And there were men on it, all dressed in blue. Did you see the sailors?"

"Yes, Punkin, I saw them . . ."

"Right under those front guns," Harding said, watching the battleship until it was a dot in the distance. "That's where they signed the surrender. I saw it in a newsreel. Right there—that's where they ended the goddamn thing."

"I was working at the plant," Mother said. "I ran a milling machine. They turned on the loudspeakers and said the war was over and that Japan had surrendered and it was better than VE Day. People yelling and screaming and kissing and throwing things in the air. I couldn't believe it. My . . . husband was in training to go to Japan. I didn't even see him after the end of the European war . . ."

She stopped then. Her voice had been running on and we were listening to her while we watched the ship until it was just tiny smoke streaks on the horizon and I looked up and saw she was crying.

"Wasn't it wonderful?" She wiped her eyes. "When it was all over, wasn't it wonderful?"

Harding nodded but didn't say anything.

"Was I very bad last night?" she asked suddenly.

He shook his head. "Not you—it was them. They didn't understand everything and were treating you wrong when they danced. Those things happen. Some asshole had whiskey and was spiking the beer with it when they opened the cans. I think you got some of that and you were gone pretty fast. Then Kowalski—well, it was just one of those things. Forget it."

She nodded and turned back into the cabin, and I thought maybe it wasn't right for her to be asking Harding if she had been bad, that maybe she should ask me or wait and ask Father when we saw him. Father would probably have killed Kowalski and maybe Harding, too.

But the *Missouri* had just been there and there was still a little smoke in the air from it. I couldn't think of anything else for very long and went back to looking for it, thinking that maybe when I grew up I would be a sailor on a battleship and look down on small ships when we went by, and I would smile and wave in my blue dungarees.

Nineteen

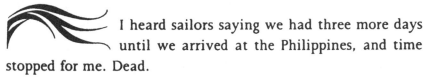 I heard sailors saying we had three more days until we arrived at the Philippines, and time stopped for me. Dead.

I could not get it to move.

I went to the front of the ship and watched dolphins. They were different kinds from the ones I'd seen before, smaller and faster, but they swam the same way, one over one over, out ahead and fast as bullets through the water.

I went to the rear and watched the sharks following, but they didn't show as well as the dolphins and weren't as active and they made me think of the plane wreck.

I colored, but all I had left were two Mary Piffles coloring books. They were all about a girl who could make herself small, and it was boring because she didn't ever do anything but get small and then turn back to big and surprise people, and I didn't like to color girls anyway. So coloring didn't help.

Mother and Harding spent more time together and seemed to always be looking at each other or touching each other and seeming sad, the way Mother had been sad with Uncle Casey, so I couldn't be with her.

I ran around the ship, looking for new things to do. There were none. I went up to the bridge and steered the ship for a while one day, but the captain was gruff and not as happy as he'd been before Mother gave all the stuff to the children on Okinawa so that didn't last and, finally, finally, I just sat.

For one whole day.

The day before we were due to arrive the ocean suddenly seemed to come alive with boats and ships.

I saw destroyers, one submarine, an aircraft carrier that looked larger even than the *Missouri* but not as full of power, but all the ships were at some distance; none of them came as close as the *Missouri*. There were smaller boats as well, some strange wooden boats with raised bows and large arms sticking out that Harding said were fishing boats out from the islands, but again, they were never close.

We were scheduled to arrive in Manila in midmorning and the night before we were to arrive Mother and I packed everything we wouldn't need the next day and then Mother left me alone for a time and went down to the dispensary to talk to Harding. She didn't tell me that, but I knew and I lay awake and tried not to think about it the way I had tried to not look at the people the sharks had hit, and finally she came back into our cabin.

She kissed me and went to bed and all the while I pretended to be asleep, but I heard her crying in the lower bunk. Not really hard, but crying, then she said, softly, "Damn, damn, damn . . ." and I didn't hear anything more.

I was awake well before dawn and in fact I had not slept soundly when I did go to sleep. The ship had moved evenly all night, the engines rumbling through the sides of the bunk, but the thought of getting at last to the Philippines, of seeing my father for the first time other than in pictures, all of it was close now and kept roaring through my brain and I only dozed in bits and pieces.

I slid out of the bunk quietly and left the lights off. Mother slept, her breathing even and deep, and I pulled my shorts on and a T-shirt and crept out of the cabin onto the deck.

Except for the lights of the ship it was still dark. I made my way to the front of the ship and stood leaning against the flaring bow and tried to see ahead, but it was impossible. There was no moon and though the sky was growing gray along the edge, it did not give much light yet.

But I could smell it.

The air had changed. It wasn't the same as Hawaii or Okinawa. There was a thickness now, a rich thickness that came across the bow, with living things in it, and rot. It smelled . . . green.

Like the dark green in a box of crayons looked, that's how it smelled to me—thick and green so you couldn't see through it; smelled green with birds and plants and leaves and a kind of mustiness and heat.

The air coming over the front of the ship felt like a warm, land shower, so thick it was, and I stood there while the light came and they slowed the ship, stood for over an hour, and as soon as it was bright enough to see anything I saw islands.

Thick and dark and low, some of them, in the faint light of morning, then richer and greener as it grew brighter, and some taller, with mountains on them, mountains that reached up into the clouds.

"Isn't it pretty?" Mother asked, and I turned to see her standing, wrapped in a blanket.

"It's the Philippines," I said, though I didn't know for certain. "Isn't it?"

She nodded. "Part of it, anyway. I don't know if it's where we're going. There are hundreds and hundreds of islands."

"We're going to Vanilla, aren't we?"

She smiled. "Manila, not vanilla."

"Yes, but isn't that where we're going?"

She nodded. "Somewhere near there. We're going to live in a compound near Manila. That's what Daddy said in his letters. Oh, Punkin, won't it be wonderful to see Daddy?"

"Is he going to meet us at the dock?"

She nodded. "I think so. I hope so. Otherwise I don't know where we'll go . . ."

We stood a long time without talking and the islands grew more and more until I could see individual trees and small buildings along sandy beaches. Mother went back inside the cabin and came out dressed, and I stood watching all the time.

There were boats everywhere, dozens of them. Small boats and large boats, navy ships and barges. We came into a large bay and I could see a city at the end of it and there were even more boats and ships so that our ship had to slow down to almost a crawl to keep from running into them.

Finally we stopped and sat still in the water. It was light by this time though still early in the morning, and as soon as the ship stopped we were surrounded by canoes that seemed to be filled with children, all clamoring and waving their hands.

"There's just us," Mother yelled down to them. And it was true. Except for a couple of sailors who had come on deck to tend the ropes there was nobody else showing. "We're the only ones . . ."

But it didn't stop the noise. They yelled and I waved and some of them waved, but when Mother didn't throw any money some of them gestured with their middle finger by holding the middle finger up and slowly sliding the two fingers next to it back down to reveal the one finger standing.

"Look," I said to Mother. "What does that mean when they do that?"

"Never mind," she said. "It's dirty."

"Does it mean like when the soldiers give each other the finger?"

"Yes. Now, never mind."

"Then it means fuck you—that's what the soldiers said."

"That's enough!" She shook me.

"But why are they doing that to us?"

"Because I didn't throw them any money."

"Why didn't you throw them any money?"

"Because I don't have any."

"But why?"

"That's *enough*."

So I was quiet even though I still didn't understand why they would make that with their fingers just because we didn't have any extra money to throw to them.

They were not there long and moved away when two tugboats came out from the city. They weren't really tugboats but navy boats, gray with numbers on them, that acted the same as tugboats. One of them took a rope from the front of the ship—the sailors called it a line, not a rope—and the other came around to the rear and pushed with a bulge made of rope netting on its nose.

The tugboats guided us through fishing boats and all the canoes toward the city where a big dock came out away from the shore.

When we were close to the dock and barely moving the tugboat at the rear pushed us in sideways, right against the dock, and the sailors tied us to the large cleats on the dock and I didn't see any of it.

I was looking at Manila.

As the ship drew closer it was possible to see the city, and it was the same as seeing the battleship.

I had seen only newsreels of war, small pictures from distances and only in black and white.

Manila had been in war and it was still there, the signs of it. Somehow everything looked blown to pieces. There was a large building that I could just see from the dock—not a skyscraper, but a large building with many floors and windows. The windows were all empty and the interior floors had been blown away so that you could see through the whole building like looking through a net. On one side, the side I could see best, there was a hole, one hole blown out where you could have put a whole house. Rubble lay everywhere and the street, the road leading away from the dock, was cratered with holes, some so large they would hold a truck easily, and in all places, jammed and packed in the rubble and on the road and the dock, everywhere there were Filipino people.

It was already very hot and most of them were dressed in shorts and loose white or khaki shirts. The women were dressed in either tight skirts or loose wraparound skirts and blouses and they all, the men and women and what seemed like thousands of children, all of them were coming at the dock toward the ship.

Twenty

Mother had brought our suitcases out and put them on the deck. We also had a trunk, but the sailors were going to bring that out from a lower hole in the side of the ship. They did that as soon as the ship was tied to the dock, carrying the trunk down a ramp from the ship.

A gangplank was brought to the side of the ship and we went to the top of it, but Mother shook her head.

"I don't see him . . ."

I couldn't see anything at first but a sea of Filipinos, young and old. There didn't seem to be any army men and then I noticed a tall man with a khaki garrison cap at a jaunty angle on his head. He was thin in the legs and had a thin bottom but wide shoulders, and he was leaning against a jeep windshield about halfway out on the dock.

The jeep and the man both had been hidden by some baskets being carried by a group of women, heaping piles of them high over their heads, and as soon as they moved I saw him.

"There," I said. "There he is . . ." But I knew it wasn't him. I'd seen pictures of him, smiling in his uniform and a garrison hat, and he had black hair and even lips. This man was brown-haired and had thin, tight lips.

He was looking at the ship, scanning it, and as soon as he saw us he held his left arm up in a short wave and started to come up the gangplank. As soon as he moved out of the crowd I saw that he was carrying a submachine gun.

"I'm Sergeant Ryland," he said. He looked hard to me, as if carved out of stone, the smile cut into his face, and I could not take my eyes off the submachine gun. It was gray with a wooden shoulder stock and foregrip. The steel was oily and the clip sticking down shone black in the light, but the wood was scarred and dented. The clip had another clip taped to it upside down so he could pull it out fast and put the new one in. I could see a bullet sticking out the open end of the downward clip, copper nosed and blunt with the brass cartridge case looking shined and buffed. *He's killed Japs with that*, I thought. *He's aimed right at them and killed them with that gun.*

"Your husband sent me for you, ma'am. He sends his apologies, but an urgent matter came up and he couldn't be here. He says he'll meet you at your house around sixteen hundred." His eyes moved up and down Mother slowly, then down to me. He smiled, another cut in his face. "Can you carry a gun?"

My tongue stuck to the roof of my mouth. I couldn't speak. I nodded.

"Fine." He handed me the submachine gun. "You hold it here and here, and don't pull the trigger. You'll kill a Flip and then we'll never get out of here."

I didn't know what he meant, didn't know what a Flip was, but I took the gun and looked up and Mother was frowning at him.

"Are you sure it's all right for him to carry it?" she asked.

"No sweat. He's tough, aren't you?"

I didn't say anything but again tried to nod. I was still staring down at the submachine gun in my hands. It was huge. It felt longer than me and horribly, wonderfully, powerfully, mysteriously deadly. The trigger seemed to glow, seemed to have a life, and I studiously avoided it.

Ryland picked up the suitcases. They looked small in his hands and went up like they were full of feathers.

"Is there anything else?"

"The trunk," Mother said. "Down there—oh, it's gone. No, there, see, those two men are taking it over to the jeep . . ."

"Or stealing it." He whistled, shrill and so loud it almost startled me into dropping the gun. Then he yelled something in a language I didn't understand and the two Filipino men carrying the trunk stopped and looked up. They were very thin but the trunk, which I knew was heavy, seemed easy for them to handle.

He pointed to the jeep and one of the men nodded. They had already been headed in the general direction of the jeep, but now they made a straight line to the front end of it and waited for us, standing by the trunk.

"They'll want you to tip them," Ryland said. "Ten centavos each—a nickel in American money." The smile widened, went back, ended. "You don't have to tip me."

Mother nodded but did not smile, and I thought it was strange but there was something in his voice, something about the way he looked at her that made her irritated. I could tell by the way she nodded and talked to him. Her voice sounded stiff. "Thank you. I wasn't thinking of it."

Ryland looked at Mother again, up and down slowly. "Isn't that funny. I thought you were."

"I think your manner is insolent," Mother said, and I looked at her suddenly because she sounded just like a woman in a movie. "And I will report it to my husband. He is, I think, your commanding officer."

He shrugged but said nothing further and took the suitcases down the gangplank. Mother followed him and I followed her, carrying the submachine gun sideways, trying not to bump it on the sides of the gangplank heading down.

The crowd of Filipinos cleared around the sergeant, then moved back in on Mother and me. They all talked and some of them touched my hair, which was white-blond from being in the sun on the ship all that time. But they did not touch the gun and made an effort to clear a way for me.

At the jeep Mother gave each of the men who had brought the trunk a nickel. They clutched the money and moved off as if carrying something very valuable, and I wondered how a nickel could mean so much to them.

The noise was deafening. Everybody seemed to be yelling at once, all in a Filipino language, which of course I did not understand, but every so often I would hear sailors swearing, and in a moment Ryland leaned down and took the gun.

For a moment I didn't know it was him and thought somebody in the crowd was grabbing it, and I jerked it back and clutched it in my hands.

He misunderstood and laughed. "No—you don't get a gun yet. Maybe later. Maybe your old man will give you a gun. But not now, not this one. I need it."

I started to say something, tell him that it was just that I didn't understand, but he had turned away and was climbing into the jeep. He placed the submachine gun in a holder rack against the side of the fender and tied it in with a strap.

"Put the kid in back," he said to Mother. "You sit in front. And hang on."

He started the jeep motor and just as I was getting between the suitcases and trunk in the back he gunned the engine and dropped the clutch.

I was driven back and down into the seat as if kicked, saw Mother's head snap back on her neck and stay back, and ahead of the jeep was horrified to see a wall of Filipinos who seemed to be on the edge of death. Their eyes were terrified and they climbed over each other to get out of the way.

Ryland kept the jeep virtually floored, shifted, shifted again, and we were off the dock.

"Sergeant," Mother said, her voice on the edge of a scream. "Sergeant! Don't you think we should slow down?"

He shook his head. "Can't. Only way to take the craters is to keep moving fast, fly over them. Otherwise it will be so rough we won't be able to take it. Goddamn Flips."

I saw an old woman with a basket of what looked like large eggs on her head seem to fall beneath the front of the jeep. Eggs and basket went flying in a great blur and I spun in the seat expecting to see her crushed and dead on the road. Instead she was sitting on the road, surrounded by broken eggs, and as I watched her two hands came up and the fingers slid down and she kept the middle finger up on each hand and turned and spat on the ground.

We hit a crater. I was smashed into the jeep and then propelled up in the air, where I spent much of the remaining hour as we drove out to the housing area.

I wanted to see Manila, or whatever the city was we were moving through, but it was nearly impossible.

"What are the craters from?" I heard Mother ask. She had one hand on the top of the windshield and the other gripping a handle on the dashboard of the jeep. "There seem to be so many of them."

He looked at her as if she were joking and saw that she wasn't. "Bombs, shells, mines—they blew hell out of the city. There was a war here."

"I know," she said. "I know about the war . . ."

"Yeah. I'll bet you do. Was it rough for you—did you have to go without your sugar?"

Mother's lips tightened and I think she was going to say more, but we hit a new series of craters and it was all she could do to hang on. We passed the building I had seen from the ship, with the enormous hole blown in the side, and he said something about it but I only caught the last part.

". . . goddamn Japs had holed up in there. They rolled a battery of field pieces up to the street and fired right in, direct fire. Blew the little bastards out."

He seemed proud of the hole and I tried to imagine it, but I didn't yet know what a field piece was so I couldn't make the pictures. *A cannon,* I thought. *Some big cannon. And they shot the cannon at the building and it made a big hole.* But I couldn't make the pictures and then we were past it and into the city, all at the same wild pace.

There were images, but they were blurred. Most of what I saw was rubble. They seemed to have shot everything and anything, shot or blown it up. Every building had a wall gone or the roof blown off. There were wrecked vehicles all along the way on both sides of the road. Trucks and jeeps and tanks with treads blown off or neat holes blown through their sides, and I thought that all of it, the blur of it, the look of it, all made me think more of garbage than anything else.

Mother must have been thinking the same thing because she said at one point, "God, the wreckage—it's all over the place."

Ryland looked at her but went back to driving without saying anything. I thought the look must have meant he was angry, but it wasn't that because when he'd driven a little longer he looked at her and leaned over and said, "You really had no idea, did you?"

There was a small smile on his mouth, a lifting at one side, and Mother shook her head. "No."

"Didn't he tell you—in letters?"

She shook her head again. The jeep bounced in a crater and she grabbed the handle on the dashboard harder. "I saw newsreels and *Life* magazine. But nothing in color, and nothing so . . . so awful. Everything is just, just wrecked."

He nodded. "That's what war is—taking shit apart. Killing.

Blowing hell out of things. All law is gone. You grab and hold and if they don't like it you kill them. No part of war—no part is building. It's all tearing apart."

"You sound as if you like it."

"I do." He nodded and negotiated around a wrecked truck jammed nose-in against the side of the road. There was a white star on the door and the cab seemed to be full of bullet holes. Hundreds of them. "I love it. I goddamn near cried the day the little bastards surrendered. I wanted to go into Japan and rip it apart . . ."

"And now you're assigned to my husband's outfit?" Mother looked at him. "Isn't that a letdown?"

He laughed and nodded. "Yes. I guess it is." He looked sideways at her and again his eyes went up and down. "At least so far . . ."

They stopped talking then, but I had seen Mother's jaw get that hard line again and I knew she was still angry, or angry again, or more angry.

Ahead of the jeep I could see a military gate. We had come out of the main part of the city, but there were hundreds of shacks made of bits of wood or cardboard boxes and crates and metal matting with corrugated roofing held down with bricks and stone.

And thousands of people. A sea of people. Jammed in among the shacks and huts and lean-tos, sitting and walking and running and sleeping people. Children ran and played, some of them in front of the jeep, barely getting out of the way before Ryland would have run over them. And I had no doubt now that he would, after listening to him.

"So many," I said to Mother. It was the first thing I had said since leaving the ship.

"So many what, Punkin?"

"People. All the native people."

"They're called Filipinos," Mother said.

"Flips," Ryland said over his shoulder. "And there were more. The Japs killed thousands of them. Hardly looks like it, does it?"

"Filipinos," Mother repeated, giving me a stern look.

"Why are there so many?"

Ryland said something under his breath that I didn't get and Mother's face turned red, but she didn't say anything.

We had arrived at a gate. There was a high mesh fence with three strands of barbwire pointing out at the top that went off in the distance from both sides of the gate, and a short way down each side there were towers with searchlights and men with heavy machine guns.

"It looks like a prison," Mother said, but Ryland didn't answer. We looked back at the towers and the machine guns and searchlights, and she asked him directly. "Why are there towers and guns and lights?"

"Huks," he said—it sounded like he was going to spit.

"What are Huks?" I asked.

He turned. "Guerrillas."

I thought he meant apes with hair on them and I shivered, wondering if they came out of the jungle and why they would need so many guns for a few gorillas. Mother spoke again.

"I thought it was all over . . ."

"Shit." He spat off to the side. "It ain't even started. We just whipped the Japs—now there's the locals. You'll hear firing every night. They try to come through the wire."

Mother grew silent, and I was still lost in images of large apes fighting to get through the fence at us.

Ahead up a small hill I could see houses and standing at the gate was a military policeman in a khaki uniform. He was wearing a steel helmet on the back of his head and he straightened the helmet when he saw us, or saw Ryland. He was also carrying a submachine gun, though a different kind from Ryland's. It was on a sling around his shoulder and hung at his side and looked more like a tool than a gun. It was all stamped metal and had a little round housing to hold the barrel, and I found out later they were called grease guns because they looked like a tool used to grease cars.

He waved us through without stopping, and Ryland nodded to him but said nothing.

We drove up the curved road to the houses and there were no more craters and everything was kept clean. It was magical. As we went through the gate and past the fence there were no more shacks, the road was clean and neat and there were no more Filipinos.

The houses weren't like houses I had seen in Chicago or San Francisco. They were built up on stilts, three feet off the ground. Around the lower part of the wall, from the floor up about four feet, the walls were of matting woven from flat strips of bamboo, and from there to the ceiling, all around the houses, there were screens.

"They're open," Mother said. "You can see right through them."

Ryland laughed. "It's the tropics—you don't need windows here. It never gets cold."

He went past one row of houses, slowed at the second, and turned down a dusty street between two rows. Halfway down he stopped.

"Number twenty-six," he said, pointing with his chin. "That's home sweet home."

Twenty-one

Every house looked exactly the same, but there were different numbers burned over the front doors.

Mother climbed out of the jeep. She wasn't about to ask Ryland for help, and she grabbed the trunk and started to slide it from the jeep.

"Oh, what the hell," Ryland said. He swung his legs out of the jeep and went around back to help her. In moments he had the suitcases and the trunk up the steps and on the small porch.

"Your servant, ma'am," he said, tipping his hat and moving back to the jeep. "Welcome home."

He drove away without looking back, and Mother and I stood on the steps. At first there didn't seem to be any other people living in the housing area. When the dust settled after Ryland's jeep, there was a moment of quiet.

Then the morning was cut by a wild scream from next door—it sounded like a woman screaming—followed by another woman's voice yelling, "You ever touch me there again and I'll kill you, you little son of a bitch."

The door opened on the house next to ours and a small woman with dark black hair came out on the porch in a halter top. She stopped when she saw us.

"Oh—hi. I heard somebody was moving in." She smiled. "You're the new people . . ."

Mother nodded. "Hi."

"I'm Lois," the woman said, "and that scream you heard was Harold. He keeps trying to touch my—well, never mind. But I'll kill him if he doesn't stop."

Mother didn't say anything. I thought Harold must be her husband, and I wondered if it was her nice tits or her cunt Harold wanted to touch. I'd heard all about that while shooting craps and playing poker with the soldiers on the ship. I did not know what a cunt was but knew that men wanted to touch it and see it a lot. It was just about all they talked about when they gambled. Tits and cunts and the fucking dice.

"Harold," Lois said, looking at Mother, "is my husband's pet monkey. He's on a wire and chain in the backyard and if I get close to him he tries to touch me. I hope the little bastard dies. By the way, don't get near him, the son of a bitch bites, too."

And she was gone. All the while she had been talking she had walked down her steps and pulled a bicycle out from beneath the house. It was painted olive-drab and had a basket and fat black tires. She threw a leg over it and pedaled off on the dirt road at a good clip.

I couldn't ride a two-wheeler and envied her ability and watched her until she was out of sight.

I don't know how long we stood that way. She was well out of sight and still we had not moved, and I looked up. Mother was standing with her hand on the doorknob, but she hadn't turned it. She was looking out across the open area to the boundary fence and the towers with machine guns and her eyes were moist and she shook her head.

"I don't know, Punkin—I don't know."

And I knew what she meant because I think I was feeling some the same way. It was all still very exciting, but there was something else to it as well, some edge of something I did not understand. It had to do with war. There was so *much* of it, so much of everything destroyed and shattered and full of holes, so much of craters in the road, so much of something hard in Ryland and the towers and the heat—it was all so much of something different that it made me not just excited but a little afraid as well, and I wished I had Dog. For a second I couldn't think what had happened to him, and then I remembered the little girl on the ship and how she had cuddled Dog and held him. And I remembered how Mother said it would be all right to give Dog to her even though I wasn't so sure of it. But I missed him now and held Mother's hand as she turned, crying, and opened the door. And we walked into our new home.

Twenty-two

The house had inner walls but no outer ones. It was very strange. We entered a small hall and there was a kitchen to the left and a bath and two bedrooms straight ahead and a large living room to the right. It was furnished with wrapped rattan furniture and solid tables and chairs, and every room had at least one wall on the outside, made up of mesh and screen with a rolled-up bamboo slat shade that could come down and cover the window.

The ceilings were high with exposed wood and beams, and just as I dropped my eyes from looking at them I saw something move. It was in the living room and when I looked again I saw that it was a lizard, hanging upside down from the ceiling, and when I looked some more I saw that they were all over the place. They were about two inches long, some close to three, and there were dozens of them, stuck everywhere. Mother hadn't seen them yet and I tugged at her slacks.

"Look at the ceiling," I said. "It's got lizards . . ."

"What?"

She looked up and stood, stunned. I had never seen her this

way. Always there was some reaction—I had heard her scream, cry, swear, laugh—but never just stand.

"Lizards," I said. "See them? They're all over the place."

"Too much," she whispered at length. "It's too goddamn much. Not lizards. Not on the ceiling. Not in *my* house."

She ran to the kitchen and rummaged in what turned out to be a broom closet. There was a strange broom made of soft bristles arranged in a fan and stuck to a short handle. She couldn't reach the ceiling with it.

She found a mop and used a piece of string from one of the bamboo window shades to tie the mop handle to the broom, which made it long enough.

"Look out, Punkin . . ."

She started sweeping the ceilings. Lizards rained down, dropping on the furniture, the floor, and as soon as they hit they ran to the walls and climbed, headed back for the ceilings. I was almost run over when two or three of them dropped in Mother's hair and she ran to the sink in the kitchen to strip them out. In a moment she was back, sweeping at the lizards with her hair tangled around her shoulders, her jaw set, the lizards falling and running back up the wall, and a voice suddenly came from the doorway.

"What in hell are you doing?"

And I turned to see my father.

I knew instantly who it was, who it had to be, because I'd seen pictures of him. All the pictures were in uniform and he was in uniform now so there was no doubt it was him. My father.

But as with the pictures of the war, the pictures of my father did not show the whole man of him, did not show a father but small black-and-white images of him.

He was huge, so tall he seemed to fill the doorway. He was wearing khakis with his hat off. His hair was black and gently wavy. He had brown eyes and he was smiling.

He said again, "What in hell are you doing?"

"Lizards," Mother said. "They're all over the goddamn place and oh, darling, I wanted to look good for you after all this time and here I am with tangled hair and my makeup all messed and Jesus Christ it's good to see you . . ."

She ran to him, reached up, and wrapped her arms around his neck and kissed him really hard, harder than I ever saw her kiss Uncle Casey or Harding, and Father kissed her back, just as hard, and kind of bent her over backward so he held her up while he kissed her all so romantic and mushy it might have been in a movie.

I just stood.

My mouth had been open and I closed it and stared at him. They kissed for a long time, then kissed again, and he held her tight and stood and looked over her shoulder at me.

"Do you know who I am?" he asked.

"You're my father." I nodded. "I saw pictures of you. Mother had them."

"Well, don't you come to hug your father?"

I nodded but my feet didn't move, couldn't move.

"Come on, Punkin," Mother said. "It's all right."

I nodded again but still did not move. I had thought of this, wondering what it would be like to see him, my father, and I had fantasized all sorts of things. I would run to him, he would scoop me up, he would have boxes of toys and candy for me and a puppy for me and a pony and here he was, standing, and I could not get my feet to move.

"What's the matter?" he asked. "Are you shy?"

I nodded, but it wasn't just that. I was frightened, and I did not know why I was frightened.

Mother turned, took my hand, and pulled me close to Father.

He leaned down. "Are you afraid?"

I nodded again.

"Can I get a hug?"

Once more I nodded. I held up my arms and he reached down

and lifted me, lifted me like nothing, like air, and held me against his chest and hugged me. I smelled his aftershave lotion and felt the bristle of his whiskers on my cheek and the feel of the starched khaki collar around his neck.

There was a second, part of a second, when he felt like a stranger, when it felt wrong to have him hugging me, then it was over and I hugged him, threw my arms around his neck and hugged and hugged.

"We came on a ship," I said, leaning back to look at his face. "And a plane crashed and the sharks killed them and we went to Okinawa and I had chicken pox and . . ."

He laughed. "Later. We'll talk about all those things later. There'll be time for all of it later—we've got all the time in the world now. All the time we need."

And because I was young and didn't know any better I believed him.

Twenty-three

The lizards were not to be harmed. They ate mosquitoes and flies and were good luck and the fact that Mother had injured and perhaps killed some with the broom might mean that bad luck was on the house or on Mother unless she crossed herself three times, which she would not do because she was not a Catholic, and this all became part of our lives, but we didn't know it yet. We would not know it until Mother and Father hired Maria and Rom.

For the moment it was hard enough for me to get used to Father, to having a father. That first day he had come home for a time and spent the middle of the day with us, talking with Mother and holding me, and I kept staring at him.

It was different from Casey. This was really my father, and I didn't have to call him Uncle, and I wondered if I was going to look like him when I grew up.

My hair was blond, almost completely white from the sun, and his was thick and black. The bathroom was the only enclosed room in the house and there was a mirror—Mother hated it because she said it was too small—bolted to the wall above the sink. There was a metal bathtub and I found that by standing on the edge of the tub I could just see myself in the mirror.

I stared at Father and then I would run to the mirror to see if any of the same things were there. I thought maybe the nose, but it was hard to tell. My nose was sunburned and had peeled and repeeled until Mother made me wear the bandage over it. This left a white band that gave me a look of perpetual surprise and made it hard to tell the true shape of my nose.

"What are you doing?" Father had seen me staring and running back and forth to the mirror, and he looked around the bathroom door.

"I want to see if we look alike."

He smiled. "It might not show yet. You're pretty blond."

"I want to look like you," I said. "Mother says I look like my uncle George. I don't want to look like an uncle. Not any uncle. I want to look like you."

His face grew serious for a second, part of a second—as if something had hurt him—and he said, "I want you to look like me, too. But we'll just have to wait and see."

"Is it because we've been apart that I don't look like you?"

He shook his head. "No. It's just that your mother has strong blood . . . Don't worry about it."

Then he picked me up again and took me back into the living room. Mother was unpacking and she looked up when we came in. "Punkin, guess what?"

"What?"

"You're going to have your own room."

"I am?"

I had never heard of such a thing. I had cousins on farms in Minnesota and they were sometimes three and four to a room. And in the apartments I always slept in the same bedroom as Mother, except when Uncle Casey was there, of course.

"Which one is it?"

"The second one down the hall."

There were two bedrooms and I ran to the second one. There was a bed with a frame over it for mosquito netting, which was all bundled at the top, and one dresser and one footlocker with army writing on it. The writing was all numbers with letters mixed in. I couldn't read them because they made no sense but traced them with my fingers and wondered if having the footlocker in my room made me a soldier and if the numbers and letters belonged to me. Through the screen I could see banana trees between us and the house next door, and it made the room look like it stood in the middle of the jungle.

"Isn't it nice?" Mother had come up in back of me, and I nodded.

"What is the netting for?"

"Each night when we tuck you in Father says we have to make sure the netting is down so you don't get bitten by mosquitoes. The mosquitoes here carry malaria."

"What's that?"

"A sickness."

"Like pneumonia?" I had had pneumonia two times and had to live in the hospital in a tent I could see through and did not want to get sick that way again. The doctors had told Mother I was dying and they sent a priest in, and she threatened to kill him and to kill God if they didn't leave me alone. She swore and screamed and didn't think I had seen it or remembered it because I was so sick, but I had. I remembered it all, and I thought she could have done it, killed the priest and killed God if she wanted to, she was so mad.

"Sort of the same. But don't worry, the netting will stop them."

The rest of that day we unpacked and Mother cleaned, and while she was doing dishes Father sat drinking a beer out of an olive-drab can and talked to us. The house came complete with dishes, a can opener, forks and knives and spoons all stamped with a big U.S. on the handles. There were even cups like we'd had on the ship, made of some kind of chips pressed together, which I thought looked nice but I knew Mother hated.

"You won't have to do any further housework," Father said. "Tomorrow the housegirl and boy will be here, and they'll take over the household duties."

He sat straight and talked in an even tone, and I still kept staring at him when he wasn't looking. He was very straight and stiff and proper-sounding. *Household duties.* He made it sound so . . . military.

"You mean we have servants?" Mother asked.

"Yes. I have already hired them. The boy is named Rom and the girl is named Maria . . ."

"Boy, girl," Mother said. "Are they children?"

Father shook his head. Once left, once right. I ran into the bathroom and did the same thing, looking in the mirror. Once left, once right. But it didn't look the same.

"They are both in their twenties," Father said, his voice carrying into the bathroom. "The terms housegirl and houseboy are simply what they call servants."

"I've never had servants before." Mother's voice had an uncertainty to it. The way she'd sounded on the steps of the house when she said she didn't know—that it was all different and she didn't know.

"It's done here," Father said. His voice was flat, almost toneless. "They're already hired and all you have to do is give them orders. They'll help with the boy as well."

It was the first time he said it, called me "the boy." Not a name, just "the boy." He did not say it in a bad way but almost as if it were my given name. "The boy," he said, and it was what he would always call me.

He stood. "I have to get back to the company for an hour or so. When I come back we'll want to eat. There should be some food in one of the cupboards. I told Ryland to handle it."

"What does Ryland do?" Mother asked. "In the company, I mean?"

Father smiled. "Whatever needs to be done. He's an old Asia hand, fought through the war here. He was a private on Corregidor and escaped and fought with hill people all through the war. He's . . . tough. Very tough."

"He's an asshole."

Strangely, Father's smile widened. "Yes. He is that. And worse. But he gets things done and in a rough way he's dependable."

I saw Mother's back stiffen. "I don't want to see him again."

Father had his hand on the knob and he turned to look at her. The smile was gone, but his eyes weren't hard. "It's different here," he said. "It really is. Back there, in the States, you saw none of the war. Europe, here, all over the world it's different . . ."

"That's what he said," Mother said. "Ryland. You sound just like him."

He shrugged. "You'll have to change, have to understand . . ."

"I still don't want to see him again."

"I'll try. But he's in my unit. There will be times . . ."

He leaned over and kissed her on the mouth, a light kiss, and looked down at me.

"There are rules," he said, his voice straight, flat again. "You cannot leave the housing compound alone, and you must be in this house with your hands washed and ready for dinner at five o'clock. If you don't know the time listen for the cannon. At exactly five o'clock every night they fire the cannon for retreat and you will be in and washed by that time. If you don't get in within the proper time limits you will be restricted."

He closed the door and was gone, and I wondered how I was supposed to know *before* the cannon went off exactly *when* it was going to go off, and what if I was playing outside too far from the house to make it when the cannon did actually fire?

But it didn't matter. I wasn't sure I was going to ever leave the house, or if I did go outside I would never leave the yard, let alone go outside the compound. The mosquitoes would get me and I would get sick and have to live in the hospital in a clear tent and watch Mother get mad and maybe kill God.

And where did they fire the cannon and could I watch? I had never seen a cannon fired except in the newsreels. But then if I went to where they fired the cannon and watched I would never be able to get to the house in time to wash my hands and avoid a restriction.

Mother was standing looking at the closed door with a strange look on her face, thinking. Except she looked kind of mad, too.

"What's a restriction?" I asked.

She jumped, startled by the sound.

"It means you can't go out," she said.

"Well, fine. I don't want to go outside anyway."

She looked down. "Don't you worry, Punkin. Don't you worry at all. He won't be doing any restricting around here . . ."

I thought it was strange that she seemed so mad at Father when she had just seen him for the first time in all those years.

But there were new screams outside, louder than before, and I ran to the back door to see what was happening.

Twenty-four

The houses were placed in neat rows along gravel streets with backyards fenced in by woven bamboo matting. There was no space between one backyard and the backyard on the next row, no alley, and the matting was not woven tight enough to provide privacy. It was possible to see through them, and I opened the back door on our house just in time to see a fat woman with short blonde hair hit a small Filipino man with a thin bamboo switch.

"Goddamn you nigger, you don't go stealing shit from me and get away with it . . . ."

Mother had come to the door with me and grabbed my shoulder.

The Filipino man was standing on the back porch of the house. It was a rough wooden porch that mirrored ours, stuck out into the yard on stilts, and had rattan chairs and a woven table on it.

The woman hit him two more times and he just stood, as the switch came down across his shoulders and onto his chest. He just stood and looked at her.

"Goddamn you nigger," she said again, in exactly the same tone. "I ever catch you stealing again, I'll fire your black ass . . ."

She hit him hard enough the second time so that I could see a welt form on the side of his neck, a white-line welt that grew as I watched, but he didn't move, didn't bend. His eyes were open and his mouth straight and he was looking right into her eyes and he didn't flinch or move but stared at her.

"You shouldn't do that," I heard and turned to see Mother staring across the yards at the woman on the other porch. Her back was rigid.

"Who the hell are you?" The woman turned. She was sweating with the effort of whipping the man and her armpits were wet and it had come down the sides of her white blouse and made the cloth stick to her bra.

"It doesn't matter who I am," Mother said. "You shouldn't do that."

"The black son of a bitch stole three bottles of Coca-Cola from me. What do you want me to do, kiss the son of a bitch?"

"That doesn't matter. You shouldn't whip anybody . . ."

I thought the woman would say more, but she turned and stomped back into the house. The man turned, looked at Mother, and smiled.

"Are you all right?" Mother asked.

He nodded. "Her whipping is not much. The Japanese whipped much harder." He turned and followed the woman into the house and we were left standing on our porch.

"I don't understand," I said to Mother. "I heard the soldiers talking on the boat about niggers and Uncle Casey talked about them, but I thought they were all Negroes. How can it be that he was a nigger?"

Mother took my ear in her finger and thumb and twisted it. "That's like swearing—to use that word. And you know what happens when you swear, don't you?"

"Yes."

"Are you sorry?"

"Yes."

"All right . . ."

"But I still don't understand. Is he or isn't he?"

"There is no such thing as that—as a nigger. That's a stupid word used by stupid people. An ugly swear word."

"Is that woman stupid?"

Mother nodded. "Yes. As dumb as they come."

"Why did the man just stand like that and let her hit him?"

She didn't answer but pushed me back in the house and we had lunch. There were cans of food—everything was in cans, even bread and roast beef and whole chickens—and Mother opened Spam and a can of bread and we had round Spam sandwiches that made me so thirsty that I wanted to drink and drink, but when I opened the faucet on the sink to get water there was a great whooshing sound and ants came out.

There were hundreds of them, a stream of them, pushed out by the air pressure and then the water.

"Look," I said to Mother. "There's bugs in the faucet."

"What?"

"Bugs—big ants. They're coming out of the faucet." I pointed and brushed my finger too close to the edge of the sink and four or five of them latched on.

They bit hard, deep, and took meat with a twisting motion that left a hole and immediate blood, and I screamed and ran in circles shaking my hand.

"Goddamn," Mother yelled. "Goddamn this place."

She grabbed me finally and brushed the ants away. They immediately bit her and she smashed them against a wall and dragged me into the bathroom where she turned on the bathroom sink only to have more ants come out.

This time she was ready and she let them flush out and washed them down the drain, then stuck my finger under the cold water.

"There, Punkin, just hold it there while I take care of the little bastards. I saw a bomb somewhere."

She left me and moved back into the kitchen, found a round canister bug bomb, and killed the ants by spraying them directly with the DDT. Not content with that she went around the house spraying every corner, along the walls and, finally, the ceiling.

Lizards dropped like rain. The cold water had done much to stop my pain and I ran after her, watching them squirm and die on the floor. She kept going until the bomb was empty, and we went back into the kitchen to finish our sandwiches.

They tasted of DDT so Mother threw them in an empty box from the pantry and made new ones and we sat and ate. Mother chewed with her lips tight, almost like she was mad at the sandwich, which still tasted of DDT, and I paused between bites.

"Why is it different here?"

"It just is."

"But why? Why isn't this like Chicago? Why are there ants in the faucet and people who whip people and other people who live in cardboard boxes?"

"It's the war."

I stopped asking. It seemed like everything was caused by the war, and I didn't see how it could make so many things different.

After lunch Mother changed into slacks and a white blouse and put her hair in a bandana with a knot in the front and went to work.

"It doesn't matter if we have servants," she said, half talking to herself while I looked at a magazine from one of the boxes in the pantry. It was an old copy of *Life*, from during the war, and it showed pictures of tanks and jeeps that had been blown up. I didn't know where it had happened because I couldn't read the words, but there was jungle in some of the pictures and I guessed that it was in the Philippines.

I looked up once to see Mother standing with her hands on her hips, the broom leaning against a chair, and she was looking at the living room with a smile on her face. Just on the end of her nose was a smudge of dirt and it made her look like a clown. I laughed and she came to me and hugged me.

"What's so funny?"

"You. You have dirt on your nose."

She brushed it off and hugged me again. "You know, this won't be so bad. Once it's cleaned up. It won't be bad to be here, will it, Punkin?"

I shook my head. Looking at the pictures had changed my mind. *The war,* I thought—*it was over but maybe not everywhere and maybe I could see some of it.*

I'd have to leave the yard of course, but I would be careful. All this time I'd heard about the war and never really seen it and here it was—or parts of it. The war.

The war.

It made me excited just to think about it. "I like it here," I said.

And Mother nodded and held me another moment before going back to work. "We'll be happy, won't we?"

Twenty-five

Maria and Rom were there when we awakened the next day. I do not know how long they had been there—perhaps all night. I was up at dawn, still too excited to sleep. Mother and Father had been drinking beer the night before and after that they had gotten all mushy and I had heard them making noise in their bedroom and it had gone on for some time so I didn't think they would be up early. I ran from room to room in the house, looking through the screens to see if anything was happening.

In the night I had been awakened by a sound that I had never heard before. It was a deep, bass thudding sound that went *dod-dod-dod* with a pause, then again, and again one more time, each time three or four thuds, then nothing. I wasn't sure if I'd dreamed it or not, but it hadn't come again and except for the sweep of the searchlights over the compound every few minutes nothing else had happened.

When I ran into the living room to look through the screens I saw two people on the front steps. They were sitting quietly apart, not talking, a Filipino man and woman, both much younger than Mother but much older than me.

The man saw me looking through the screen and smiled. He poked the woman and she looked up and smiled as well.

"Good morning," I said. "Who are you?"

"I am Rom," the man said, "and this is Maria. We are here to work."

"Mother and Father are still asleep. They drank beer and made noises last night so I don't think they'll get up early."

Rom nodded. "That is all right. We will wait for them. Do not wake them up."

He spoke funny. The words were clear and seemed almost perfect to me, almost round, but there was an accent and he didn't run the words together. It made me think of the man on the beach in Hawaii—different, but somehow the same.

Maria said nothing, but she watched me quietly, a small smile on her lips. She had long, dark black hair that hung down her back and a small, slight body that made her seem almost tiny though she was nearly as tall as Rom. Her eyes were huge, brown, and lifted slightly at the corners. She was wearing a flowered, wraparound skirt and a white blouse that looked both wrinkled and very clean.

Rom was also thin, and I thought then that all the people by the boat and all the people we saw coming through the city had looked thin. I hadn't seen any fat Filipinos. Rom had thick hair on top but cut short on the sides and long, thin arms with muscles that seemed to be ropes under the rich brown skin. He was wearing loose pants and a white T-shirt with a hole in the shoulder so his skin showed there and it was also brown and rich looking.

"What is your name?" Rom asked.

I told him and he nodded.

"But Mother calls me Punkin," I added.

"What does that mean? What is punkin?"

"A punkin is a large orange thing you cut eyes and a mouth in for Halloween."

"Halloween?"

"It's when you go around to get candy from people."

"And you look as this looks—this punkin?"

I shook my head. "No. Mother just calls me that. I don't know why."

At that he nodded and seemed about to say something more, but a voice came from behind me.

"Who are you talking to?"

I turned and Father was there in his pants and an undershirt. He was holding a pistol. I hadn't known that he had one, but it was there. A large gray automatic pistol, square, and it filled his hand. The barrel was half aimed at the floor, half up toward me and the screen. His finger was on the trigger.

"These two people," I said. "They're Rom and Maria. They're here to work."

He came forward then, two steps, until he could see them through the screen. The gun was up, the barrel aimed at them.

"You have papers," he said. It was flat, not a question but something more. An order. He was not smiling. The barrel of the pistol seemed very steady, pointed right at Rom's chest.

I was fascinated—on the edge of fear and horror—but it didn't seem to bother Rom to have the gun pointed at him. He nodded. "I have."

Maria did the same. "In my bag."

I saw then that they each had a bundle. They seemed to be made of sheet or canvas, the four corners tied together to contain whatever was inside.

"Let me see them," Father said. "Hold them up to the screen."

Rom held a small sheet of thick paper up to the screen. Father leaned forward, pushing me sideways, and read the paper. Maria rummaged in her bag and I saw the barrel of the pistol swing to cover her.

He can't shoot her, I thought. *How can my father shoot a woman?*

She brought the same kind of paper out and held it to the screen.

"What's the matter?" Mother came through the bedroom door and into the hallway. Her hair was tousled and hung in her eyes.

Father didn't say anything.

"These two have come here to work," I said. "They are Maria and Rom."

"Why do you have a gun?" she asked Father.

"Because I had to check them first," Father said. He spoke without looking at her, his eyes on Rom and Maria. The gun was still up, aimed somewhere between them. "There was perimeter activity last night—didn't you hear the machine guns?"

"Is that what the sound was?" I asked.

He nodded. "That means somebody was trying to break into the compound."

"And they shot them?"

Father didn't answer. He turned to Mother. "Sometimes they break into the compound to steal things and sometimes to make raids. They have to be stopped."

Mother stepped forward. I could tell she was angry. Her back became stiff when she grew angry and it was stiff now.

"I don't think they would break into the compound to sit on our front steps, do you?"

She moved around Father and motioned through the screen. "Come to the front door."

Maria and Rom grabbed their bundles but did not stop at the front door. Instead they went around to the back and waited on the back porch.

Mother gave Father a short look.

Father watched her go, then looked down at me and smiled. "I guess she told me, didn't she?"

I was staring at his hand. "I didn't know you had a gun."

He nodded. "You must never touch it or play with it." He pushed a button and the clip dropped out of the handle. I could see the round nose of a bullet and the brass of the cartridge case sticking out from the top of the clip, shiny and catching the light.

He pulled the slide back and ejected another bullet that had been in the barrel, then handed me the empty gun. "Here, hold it if you like."

I took it and the weight of it pulled my hand down. There was writing on the top of the barrel slide. "What does it say?"

He leaned over. "It says 'Colt .45, patented 1911.' And then a serial number."

I tried to hold it up with one hand and aim out the window, but it was too heavy and I had to use two hands. "I carried Sergeant Ryland's tommy gun yesterday when we left the ship."

"You did?" Father smiled. "Usually nobody gets to touch that gun. It goes everywhere with him. He's had it since he was in the jungle—carried it all through the war."

He took the pistol, put the clip back into the handle, and turned as Mother came into the room with Rom and Maria.

"Let's start over," she said. She introduced us formally—I saw Father smile again but hide it with his hand—and we each shook hands. Rom leaned down to shake my hand, but Maria touched me on the cheek. Her hand felt warm and dry.

"Now, I've never done this before," Mother said. "Had servants, I mean. So explain it all to me."

Rom and Maria stood silently off to the side and Father gestured to them. "They are screened and hired by the administrative office. Of course you can turn them down if you don't like them, and if you do they are immediately released and their papers are revoked. There are many others waiting to get jobs so letting them go doesn't present a problem."

"Except for them," Mother said.

"Well, yes, I guess so. Except for them."

"How much do we pay them?"

"They each get three dollars a week and room and board."

Mother stared at him. "Three dollars a *week?*"

Father nodded. "That's the going rate. Their wage is deducted from my pay, and they are paid by the administrative office."

"That's not enough."

Father shook his head. "You can't give them more."

"The hell I can't."

"It will . . . confuse things for everybody if you do."

"You mean the others might have to do the same?"

He nodded. "It's a delicate situation."

"Well, isn't that just too goddamn bad?" Mother said. "I'm not going to have somebody cleaning my house for less than fifty cents a day. That's slavery."

I could have told Father to stop. I'd seen her like this before. Her back was stiff, and even with her hair all messed from sleeping and a housecoat wrapped around her she looked ready to fight.

He must have seen it as well because he sighed and nodded. "All right, all right—how much?"

Mother smiled sweetly. "Well—whatever is fair. What can we afford?"

They went back and forth with Rom and Maria and me standing there, and finally Father agreed to five dollars a week each, which Mother still thought was not enough. But she finally nodded.

"Now, where do they sleep?" She asked when the money talk was done.

"Most people," Father said quietly, "let them spread a pad in the back entryway."

"On the floor?"

"I didn't think it would be adequate." Father sighed. "Perhaps we could just rent a house for them?"

Father knew when he was whipped, and he left the rest to Mother and dressed and went to his office. I wondered what he did. I thought of him just going to work with the army, maybe shooting guns or driving a tank. But he wore such good clothes that it didn't seem possible. He dressed in clean, crisp khakis and went to the door. Magically, Ryland appeared in the jeep and saluted as Father walked out and they drove off together.

Mother finished dressing, wrapping her hair in a red bandana, and all this time Maria and Rom stood in the middle of the living room and waited while I stood watching them.

"Well," Mother said, coming out of the bedroom when she'd finished dressing. "Let's get started, shall we?"

I'm not sure what Rom and Maria expected, but I know it wasn't Mother. She worked right alongside them and had me doing it as well. We took all the furniture out of the house and set it on the walkway and we swept, cleaned, and mopped everything, even the walls.

That's when we learned about the lizards. Mother had missed some and she saw one in the corner of the ceiling and went after it with a broom.

"No!" Maria screamed. "Do not hurt it . . . They bring luck to a house."

"It's a lizard," Mother said. "A goddamn lizard on my ceiling. That's supposed to be lucky?"

Maria insisted and Rom came into it as well. He was carrying a chair outside, and he stopped and put himself between Mother and the lizard.

"Please," he said. "They eat mosquitoes. Do not kill him."

And to my surprise I saw that Maria was starting to cry and that Rom had tears in the corners of his eyes as well.

Mother put the broom down. She had made coffee—it was powdered coffee in a can, but she had made a full pot—and she poured three cups, one for each of them.

"I don't understand," she said. "Why it is so important—the lizards being on my ceiling."

Rom and Maria stood holding their cups. They looked uncomfortable.

"Tell me," Mother said. "Tell me why."

Maria bit her lip but said nothing. Rom stood and shook his head, but Mother still waited and at last he coughed and cleared his throat.

"It is us," he said. "The lizards are our friends, a way we do things. The Japanese would not allow us to do anything that belonged to us. They made us do . . ."—he looked at Maria and at me and then away quickly—". . . many things that we did not want to do. One of the things they forced us to do was kill and eat the lizards raw." He stopped.

It was very quiet in the kitchen. The icebox motor started and it made me jump.

Mother looked at Maria and her eyes became soft. She stepped forward and touched Maria's hair. I didn't understand any of it, why lizards would make her touch Maria like that or why Mother's eyes would get tears, but she smiled and nodded.

"We won't hurt the lizards," she said. "Even if they drop in my soup . . ."

And nobody said anything more about it, but I looked at Maria and Rom, saw their eyes, and knew that they would do anything for Mother from then on.

Twenty-six

We settled in within a week or so, or as much as we could. For me it meant exploring the small backyard, which had some scruffy, bent-over banana trees and wooden chairs. The yard was closed in with the cane matting, but even so I could see the yard next to us.

And the monkey.

I had never seen a monkey, not even in a zoo. The people next to us were named Nickerson, and they called the monkey son of a bitch. I never heard them use another name for it, and they never seemed to talk to it without yelling. It was always, "Come here and eat, you little son of a bitch," or "The little son of a bitch shit on the table again." Always in a yell if it was the man, who was shorter and more round than Father but the same rank, and in a shrill scream if it was the woman, whom we had met when we first arrived.

I learned to hate the monkey. He was small, wiry, and covered with sparse gray fur. He was half bald except for bushy eyebrows, which he seemed to be able to slide back onto the top of his head.

They kept him on a long chain that was in turn fastened with a ring to a wire that allowed the monkey—by the end of the first week I always called him the little son of a bitch unless Mother or Father were listening—free range in his own backyard. He could even climb the matting and come down on our side of the fence if he liked to do so.

The little son of a bitch quickly discovered me and found that I would run if he came at me with his eyebrows pulled back on top of his head and his teeth bared, screeching and throwing handfuls of dirt and stones at me.

It was like having a monster in the next yard, waiting for me to come out the back door. For some reason whenever I went in to tell Mother and she went out to look, the monkey would be back on his side of the fence, playing dirty with himself, something he seemed to do almost constantly, or picking at the scattered hair on his stomach.

"Oh, don't worry, Punkin," Mother would say, "he's just playing."

But I knew he wasn't playing and that the little son of a bitch would really like to take a chunk of meat out of me. Finally I caught the little son of a bitch square across the head with a piece of wood I found under the back steps and it slowed him. After that I never went into the yard unless I had the piece of wood with me.

My fear of the outside world diminished rapidly with controlling the monkey and by the end of the second day the yard had become boring. I explored the front yard, up and down the dirt street a hundred yards or so, and within ten days I was all over our part of the housing compound.

The houses were all in neat rows and the rows arranged so that the houses formed a squarish block of perhaps twenty homes. They were almost all empty except for the little cluster our house was in, and I saw no other children. This block of homes lay in the middle of a large, grassy meadow built on the side of a shallow slope and was close—less than a quarter-mile—to the boundary fence and watchtowers.

But the housing compound we lived in was just the edge of a much larger fenced-in military reservation. On the other side of the small incline it stretched for miles, with some other housing areas—these, I found, were also for military dependents but were mostly empty—and in the distance there were larger buildings and a water tower. At the base of the water tower, barely discernible in the distance, there was a flagpole and at the base of the flagpole was the retreat cannon. At five o'clock every evening, as Father had said, a group of soldiers in freshly pressed uniforms blew taps on a bugle, fired the cannon, and brought the flag down.

I was to see this later, many times, but at first I expanded my limits only to the top of the incline behind our own smaller housing compound and held there. It was possible to see many things from the top of the hill—trucks moving in the more military area under the water tower and planes flying and landing farther away at an airstrip. In the open area between where I stood and the water tower were large grass-covered fields and great open areas full of wrecked equipment. There were tanks, small beetle-looking things, and odd-looking trucks and scrap, garbage, and bits of metal everywhere. It was a place that seemed to have been blasted, blown to bits, and I asked Father one day why all the junk was scattered there.

He was so, so straight, my father, so stiff and proper and military, and he rarely spoke to me except to give orders or tell rules. Sometimes he would wink and smile, especially when Mother chewed him out, but he rarely talked to me at any length. This time was different.

"Some Japanese were caught there in the open by the fly-boys," he said. "They bombed the whole place to pieces. I talked to one of the pilots and he said they had to back up and get in line so they could take turns dropping on them . . ."

"That's enough," Mother said. We were sitting in the kitchen eating. "He doesn't need to hear that."

Father looked at her and shook his head. "I guess not. Sometimes I still forget that it's over."

From then on if I asked about something to do with the war, he never answered in specifics and frequently didn't answer at all. I had many questions. Buildings that had been blown down, signs with painted skulls that I could not read, and one place where the perfect outline of a person was blasted into a wall. But with one exception he never answered except in generalities.

The exception was at a place called Sandiago Prison. One day after we'd been in the Philippines about a month, Father came home and said that we were going to visit a place where the Japanese had kept prisoners during the war.

"I had a friend there," he said. "A man I knew before the war. I was assigned to Europe and he got the Pacific. They've just opened the prison and I thought I should see it."

He did not insist that we go, though I wanted to—anything to do with the war was fascinating to me. Strangely, Mother said that we should go.

"If you knew him . . ."

"Where is he now?" I asked. "The friend?"

"He didn't make it."

That's how he said it. Not he's dead, or gone. Just that he didn't make it. All the time Father was fighting in Europe and Mother worried that he would be killed I asked her about death, which I didn't understand, and she said that if it happened Father would go to sleep and never wake up and never come back from Europe.

I knew better now. The sharks had taught me on the ship, and listening to the soldiers, and I understood death a little better. But I didn't know if Father meant his friend had died or just had gone some other place. So I asked.

"Is he dead?"

Father stiffened. We were in the living room and he was walking across the floor. He stopped and seemed to grow rigid and looked at me and I was afraid and didn't know why I was afraid.

Then he softened. "Yes. He's dead. The Japanese killed him."

So we went to the prison and saw the stone walls and the places where the Japanese did things and I didn't know why Mother had let me come after we arrived. At first I just thought it was another old stone ruin. There were many of them, almost everywhere you looked—at least what I thought were old ruins but they were really buildings, some of them quite new, blasted and destroyed and made to look old.

And here was another. A walled-in place called Sandiago Prison and it was not until we were inside and looking at things that Mother found what they were for. And then it was too late to leave because Father did not want to go.

"We have to see this," he said, taking my hand firmly. "The boy has to see this."

We went through a hall with a series of rooms. They were small with no windows, little rooms with solid steel doors, and I thought they must be cells. I had never seen a cell but had heard a radio show about a man in prison and they talked about cells and the doors clanged when they shut them and these doors looked like they would clang.

There were other people near us—soldiers. They had come in a group in the back of a truck with a canvas top. One of them mumbled, but I heard him.

"The bastards tortured them in here."

Of course I didn't know for certain what torture meant, except in general terms, but I knew it couldn't be good because the soldier sounded like he hated the Japanese for doing it and nothing good could come from these evil little rooms. But I still did not understand how it all was, how bad it had been, until we went into an open area with cells arranged around the edges.

It was a compound with a packed gravel base and large arched cells around the sides. Across each of the openings there were steel grates and Father stood looking at the grates with my hand in his, still held tightly, as if to keep me from escaping, and my other hand in Mother's hand, and he said, "This is where they had mass executions. They packed them in there, closed the grates, and turned flame throwers on them and burned them all to death."

"Oh, God," Mother said, and she didn't even tell him to stop because of me and I wish she had because I understood now, understood what had happened. The walls of the enclosures were all a brown-yellow, a greasy color, and I could see how the grates would be closed and the people would be burned and it was too much and I turned away and was sick, threw up all over my own shoes, and then cried and Mother held me and we left. But I dreamed of it for many nights and woke up with my eyes wide open and the feeling of burning on me, all over me, and the sight of those enclosures with their arched doorways and steel grates was there, always there when I awakened from the bad dreams.

Twenty-seven

Women started to come over.

Rom and Maria settled in. Rom on his bunk in the back and Maria on a bed in my room, where I could hear her at night sometimes crying softly, but I didn't know why until later. The heat, the massive heat of the tropics, was new as well and even at night it was hot and thick and I could not sleep. Sometimes I awakened in the night and would hear Maria crying softly, but when I called her name and asked if she was all right she didn't answer. I realized she was asleep, that she cried each night while she slept, all night, cried softly and sometimes murmured words that I didn't understand and after a time I became used to it but at first it kept me awake.

For some time after we arrived Mother was very close to me. She never let me out of her sight. It was Mother and me. Sometimes she even helped me color. She would start Maria on housework, which Mother always did over when Maria wasn't watching—taking small swipes with a broom or dust rag—and then she would sit with me and talk and sometimes color or draw pictures.

Then the women started to come and things began to change for Mother.

They were other officers' wives. Father had been in the army for fifteen years and so knew how the army worked. But for Mother, who had married him right before the war, it was all new.

There was then a very rigid class structure in the military. Officers' wives had certain social obligations to one another depending on the ranks of their husbands. They formed groups and card clubs—they played bridge and whist—and held tea parties. And sometimes they would drink.

As each officer's wife came and met Mother she brought a card and left it, and Father gave Mother some cards that she had to give them in return.

I managed to take several of Father's cards and though I couldn't read them very well, I had a great time carrying them around and pretending to hand them to people.

"My card," I would say to Rom, mimicking the women, and hand him the card, though he had to return it so I could use it again.

If it was strange to me it was all very new and exciting for Mother. I heard her talking to Father one night after they'd gone to bed and she sounded like a girl.

"Colonel Pleasence's wife came today to present her card," she said. "She's invited me to tea next Tuesday at the officers' club."

"She doesn't like women who smoke," he said. "Don't smoke in front of her."

Mother smoked now and then, I think because it made her look like a movie star.

"Is it that important?" I heard her ask.

"He's my commanding officer," Father said. "It can mean promotion . . ."

"Can it mean a transfer back to the States?" she asked.

"You just got here . . ."

"I know, I know. But . . . it's all so different."

"Give it time, you'll learn. You'll learn."

Sometimes they would come alone, sometimes they would come with one or two others and they would smile at me and sit and drink coffee with Mother and talk about women who weren't with them and they talked about other things. They told Mother how to get a jeep to take her to shop at the commissary or the PX, even though there wasn't much to buy there. There was no milk except for powdered milk and no ice cream and no candy and no potatoes and no meat except for canned meat and powdered chicken soup. That's what they told her. And they told her about something called ladies' night at the officers' club, where they got together and had what they called a good old time and the gin flowed like water and they laughed and planned all the good things they were going to do.

But mostly they talked about other officers' wives who weren't there, about what they did or when they did it, and still they laughed but the laughter changed then, became sharp.

At first Mother didn't seem to fit in with them. She kept forgetting she had servants and would get up to get the coffee herself or tell me to bring in the pot to pour for them.

"My dear," one of them said, a tall woman with thin wrists and thick red jewelry, "you mustn't do your own serving. What will happen?"

And Mother would sit down and Maria would bring in the coffee and pour it and when she was gone they would all talk about her.

"So nice, you know, for what happened . . ."

"Oh, yes, the Japanese you know. All the girls, even very small ones were used. Five, six years old—they didn't care. They passed them around from man to man, sometimes many men at a time. It was horrible, just horrible."

I didn't understand it, didn't know what they meant, but it

made Mother turn white when they talked about it, and I knew she had trouble thinking about it because her back got all stiff and her voice sounded flat.

"Have some more coffee," she said, her voice even and dead. "Would you like a corner sandwich?"

I thought Maria's crying when she slept must be because she had trouble with the Japanese, so one day I asked Mother.

"It's because they made her sleep with them," Mother said. "That's all. Now don't talk about it anymore and don't ask Maria anything about it or I'll paddle you blue."

Which wasn't true because Mother never hit me, ever, and it still didn't make any sense because when I slept with Mother it didn't make me cry, but I didn't say anything more about it.

As time went on Mother was gone more and more. She took to leaving me with Maria and Rom for longer and longer periods.

"The girls are coming to take me to a card party," she would say, doing her makeup and changing clothes. "I'll be back late." Or, "I'm meeting the girls at the officers' club. Maria will fix your lunch."

Maria cooked only one thing. At first I didn't like it, but later it was nearly the only thing I would eat. She boiled rice until it was just past done, sticky and thick, and she would drop a pile of this on a plate. On top of the rice she would pour the contents of an opened can of sardines—fish, oil, bits, and all. She mashed this down into the rice with a fork, handed me a spoon—she never let me eat with the same fork she used for mashing—and pushed the plate at me.

"For you," she said. "It is good."

The first time she did it Mother had gone to the club and Rom was cleaning the yard and I thought I would throw up. The smell of the fish oil became caught up in the steam from the rice and rose into my nostrils in thick streams. I could smell it in my hair for the rest of the afternoon.

"I can't eat this," I said. "It smells like fish too much."

So Maria ate it. She didn't say a word. She pulled the plate over, scowled at me, and ate every bit of it with her hands, using her fingers to kind of wipe the rice around in the sardine juice left on the plate, and licked the empty sardine can to boot.

And didn't feed me anything for the rest of the day. By dinner time I was starving and the next day, when Maria again made rice and sardines and pushed the plate over, I ate it. It wasn't so bad and by the fourth or fifth time I was licking the can the way she had done, to get the rest of the oil.

Until this time I had not been very far from the house. Just to the top of the hill. But with Mother gone most of the time and Maria busy with the house and Rom busy with the yard or helping Maria I explored farther and farther until one day I was on the edge of the bombed area.

It was more extensive than I had thought from the top of the hill. Standing on the edge it was possible to see more and there were parts of trucks and tanks everywhere, all rusted and bent and broken and many of them burned.

I thought maybe I would see some dead Japs the way I had seen them in newsreels, all bloated and sometimes floating in water on a beach, but I couldn't and I picked my way through the wreckage slowly until I was standing next to a tank.

From a distance it had looked small, almost cute, with a little turret stuck like a small hat on a toy. But up close it was larger, and ugly. One tread had been cut and unrolled so it sat on the last section and the turret was turned and the short gun barrel drooped down and I knew I was going to go inside it before I got next to it, knew it but stopped with my hand on the tread housing and felt afraid.

What was inside? What if there was a dead Jap in there, all ugly and full of holes? But I couldn't turn away and I stepped on the sprocketed bogey wheels and climbed up. The hatch on top of the turret was open and sprung back.

I leaned over and peered down inside.

It was dark and smelled damp, musty. Many of the vehicles had burned but the tank had not caught fire and the inside was unharmed. I leaned in, pulled back, leaned in a bit more, and when I couldn't see any bodies or skeletons, I climbed inside.

There was a small seat for the driver and another seat for the man who sat in the turret—I supposed the gunner—and the seats seemed almost right for me. They were all of steel, with no padding; everything in the turret was of steel and had rusted a great deal. But even with the rust and corrosion I could see the Japanese writing, and there were dials and levers and switches everywhere, or so it seemed, and I was instantly transported.

I was in the war and there were Japs in the tank and I had killed them all and I was a hero and had saved all the people in the compound . . .

"It is not for you," a voice boomed down from above, "to be inside the tank. You will become dirty."

I almost screamed, the voice frightened me so, but when I looked up it was only Rom, looking down at me and smiling.

"You scared me."

"I am sorry. But I am to watch you when your mother is not here and I cannot let you be inside the tank."

"I'm only playing."

"You are filthy. Come out. Now."

Though we had not been in the compound long I was already becoming corrupted by the system and knew that Rom was a servant and that he could not order me to do things or I could tell Mother and she could get him fired, but his voice was firm, like the steel in the tank, and I climbed out.

"See the rust," he said, clicking his tongue and pointing a long finger at me. "It is in all places on you."

I looked down and he was right. In just moments inside the tank I was completely covered with rust.

"It is inside your ears," he said, "and in your hair. Come now and we will clean you before your mother returns."

He held my hand and took me to the house where he stripped me and stood me in the metal bathtub in the bathroom and used a bucket to wash me down again and again with fresh water.

Maria stood in the door and watched, laughing and pointing at me until Rom said something in Tagalog so that she became quiet.

When I was clean it was time for lunch and Maria made me rice and sardines, which by this time I was eating, and by the time Mother came home the incident was over. Or nearly so.

"Why are your clothes wet?" she asked. I could smell the gin on her breath. It smelled like something hard, like cold steel smelled or tasted, and I hated it. She weaved slightly but had a small smile on her lips. She'd been playing cards at the officers' club and one of the other women had brought her home in a jeep. "I saw them drying on a cord in the bathroom."

"I was playing," I said, "and got dirty. Rom cleaned them."

"Oh. How nice of him. Rom?" She turned to the back of the house. "Rom? Thank you for cleaning his clothes."

But he did not come. Rom and Maria tried to avoid Mother when she had been drinking, which was more and more all the time, and they spent a lot of time in their living areas when she had the smell on her breath: Maria in my room where she was continually sewing and Rom in the back entryway where he sat, just sat, and smoked small brown cigarettes that smelled of sweat.

If they did not come they saw, they always saw, and they would watch Mother. I had seen Rom sit in the back when she had been drinking, had seen him sit and watch quietly, smoking the evil little cigarettes that he rolled in rough paper, and study her sitting in the living room and when he did this he would look sad, tired and sad, and shake his head gently. Sometimes when she came home and had been sitting for a time, her head back and her eyes closed, Rom would say something to Maria and she would take a washcloth and dampen it and go to Mother and put it on her forehead. But Rom always waited until Mother was asleep before he called Maria to do this, and until then he would sit and watch her and smoke and shake his head and seem almost to cry.

Twenty-eight

The first Christmas we were to spend in the Philippines was coming and Mother had decided to make it like a Christmas at home, back in Chicago.

"We'll use banana leaves to make a tree," she said, "and we'll cut our own tinsel from tinfoil . . ."

She started Maria and Rom doing things they didn't understand, but they worked happily, caught up in the spirit of the holiday, and I helped by painting Christmas-tree ornaments that Mother cut from empty coffee-can metal with an old pair of scissors.

But it was all for nothing. A day before she was going to make the tree Father came home early and said something quiet to Mother, in her ear, that we could not hear.

"Typhoon?" she said aloud.

Rom and Maria were helping me sort and cut thin strips of tinfoil into tinsel, and the word stopped them dead. Rom put the scissors down slowly, gently. He said nothing but watched Father quietly, his eyes intent. Maria stopped with one hand to her mouth.

"It's a big wind," Father said. "Like a hurricane. They say it will get here tomorrow."

"Here?" Mother looked around the house. "You mean here, as in the Philippine Islands, or here, as in the house?"

"The house."

"But this isn't built well enough to handle a fart . . ."

"We have to leave. There is a large building in the city and we must go there. We have until five o'clock to get out of here and to safety. After that the wind will start to rise and it will be dangerous . . ."

Rom stood suddenly. "I must go," he said. "To be with my family."

Father nodded. "Of course." He looked at Maria. "Would you rather leave or stay with us?"

"I will stay and go to the building with you." It was hard to tell what she was feeling from her eyes. The Japs had done those things to her and her eyes always looked worried or afraid, but I thought she looked afraid in a different way now. Not a memory-afraid but a now-afraid.

Rom left at once, and Mother and Maria and I began to pack. Father had to rush off to help with some military evacuation. "I'll be back with the jeep in two hours. Be ready."

"I have to have my makeup," Mother said, her hands on her hips. "And we'll need blankets and sheets and food. Maria, take all the sardines and those old ration cans—anything we can eat cold. I don't suppose we'll be able to cook."

I ran outside to see the typhoon coming, but I couldn't see anything different. There were some clouds, rain clouds, and they were darker out past the city, past Manila, but the wind wasn't very strong and I went back in to report.

"It's nothing to worry about. Just some old rain clouds . . ."

Father did not come back in two hours with the jeep. Ryland did.

"He'll meet you at the building." He said nothing more but

helped load the jeep with what we had packed on the steps and drove off with us. Mother sat in front and Maria and I were in the rear.

He drove silently until we came to the gate leaving the compound. The guards at the gate had been doubled to four men and they had a machine gun set up inside some sandbags.

"For looters," Ryland said. "After it's over. If there's anything left."

"You mean those men have to stay there through the storm?"

"They'll leave and go to bunkers at the last minute. Then come back as soon as it's passed."

"How long will it last?"

"It changes. A day, maybe two, and we can come back. I knew one that lasted three days and another one that didn't hit at all. You never know."

We steered through the shack town. Everybody was gone. Here and there a dog ran or dug into garbage, but there wasn't a person to be seen. I wondered where they went, where Rom went with his family.

Ryland drove fast but even so there was a wind starting by the time we came to the city. He turned down several side streets and came at last to a large stone building.

"Here. In the basement."

It had been a rich man's home many years before and since had been turned into offices for some kind of government work. The building was made of huge stone blocks, laid one on another and the walls were so thick the doors looked almost like tunnels.

There were people everywhere. Most of them were white, but many were Filipino, and a man in a soldier's uniform but wearing a baseball cap came out.

"Follow me."

He led us down a flight of stairs into the basement. It was all one room, so big it almost seemed like outside, and it was filled with bunks. Hundreds and hundreds of beds.

"Find a bunk," the man said. "And stick with it. There's lots more coming and you don't want to lose your place." He looked at me and Mother. "The boy sleeps with you on the same bunk."

And he was gone.

Mother took Maria and me to the far end and found three bunks. She put one of us on each one.

"But I'm supposed to be with you," I said.

"It's for your father. Just save it."

Ryland moved to a corner, well away from anybody, and sat with his back to the wall, watching, the gun across his lap.

There were Filipino children and they kept running and playing until finally I could stand it no longer and Mother said she would watch the bunk for Father and I could take off and play.

"Don't leave this basement. And check back every five minutes."

I joined the nearest group and we played follow the leader around the basement, running between bunks and generally making a nuisance of ourselves.

More and more people came until the basement was packed and Mother decided to give up Father's bunk to a woman with four children and two chickens. The chickens were tied with long cords around their legs so they could roam and they pecked at anything that looked like a bug, including my toenail if I moved my foot the right way.

It all had the air of a large park or camping ground. Everybody was friendly and tried to help one another. I played with the other children until I was tired, then I just wandered, looking at things.

The basement was deep but around the top edge there were windows, long, narrow ones that lay sideways, and men came and put up barrels with boards on them to use for scaffolding and took out all the windows. One of them told me it was so glass wouldn't blow in on us when the storm came, but I had stopped believing in the storm. They left the scaffolds and I found that I could stand on them and see out the windows.

It was just getting dark and the clouds towered now and looked black and there was some rain here and there and the wind seemed to be picking up a bit. But I had seen worse wind and hadn't run for basements and I was feeling a bit let down—I wanted to see a real typhoon now that everybody had talked about it. I went back to our bunks just as Father arrived and we ate some sardines and crackers and a can of fruit cocktail that tasted almost like candy. I had run and run and was so tired I went to sleep early, probably about six, and so I was awake when the typhoon finally hit.

I woke up because I had to pee so bad I almost wet the bed. There was a bathroom at the end of the basement and I made my way through the bunks of sleeping people. They had turned out almost all the lights and left just enough so it was possible to see. After I peed I started back for our bunks when I heard a strange sound.

Actually it wasn't a sound to hear so much as to feel—a pressure, a moan in the air that almost seemed to be inside my head.

I went to the end of the basement and climbed on top of the scaffolding and looked outside.

Dawn had come but there was no sun. The sky was gray, so dark that it seemed to be almost night, and the wind was tearing at things as it roared past. Trees, palm trees and large mango trees, were down and a banana tree across the street from the building shredded as I watched. One second it was there and then it was torn to pieces, small pieces, as the wind ripped it apart and carried it away and I turned to get down when I saw the man.

To the front of the building was a large field with short cut grass. I would have thought it was for football or baseball except that they didn't do those sports, and running across the field was a Filipino man.

He had on a white shirt, but it had come open and was blowing back from him exposing his stomach and chest, and he was running sideways across the wind, trying to get to the building. The wind was so strong now that it was tearing buildings apart, so strong that it seemed to lift the man and help him run so that he was taking giant steps, leaping and running and almost flying.

Then the tin came.

All the buildings, all the military buildings and the houses on the base had roofs made of corrugated metal. These were in long sheets and when the wind got under them it simply tore them off the roofs and sent them flying away.

They were long and jagged and as sharp as razors and when caught by the wind they moved very fast. The sky was full of them, flipping and careening in all directions, and one of them now, a whole section that had come loose, came hurtling out of the sky, driven by the wind like a flying razor, and caught the man from the side at the waist. The sharp metal hit him edge-on and cut him almost exactly in half.

The tin flipped the top half off to the side and then dropped him, and the legs and bottom half ran on for another step or two before falling and the man, the top half of the man, pulled himself around with his arms and saw his legs, his bottom half four feet away, down but the legs still moving, and he turned back, looked to the sky, and opened his mouth and screamed.

Except that the wind took the sound and his scream became the wind, mixed in the wind, and I didn't want to watch anymore and I looked down but then looked up and watched until his head fell and his hands stopped moving.

Other people were up by this time, others who had heard the wind, and somebody watching at one of the other windows, a thin man in uniform pants and a T-shirt, said, "Look at that . . ."

I looked again and saw that two other men were running out. They had a metal garbage can between them and they took the two parts of the man's body and dropped them in the can and struggled back against the wind, dragging and carrying the can with the legs and head sticking out the top.

"Fucking Flips," the man said. "Putting him in a garbage can like that. They don't give a shit about whether people live or die . . ."

But I knew the man was wrong. I knew Rom cared for me, and for his family. I went back to bed where Mother was up rubbing her eyes and I tried to tell her all about it, about the man being cut in half and the other Filipino men picking him up with the garbage can, but I started to cry before I could tell her that I knew they really cared because of Rom and his family.

She held me for a time, until the crying went down, then she put me in bed even though it was daylight and I slept until it was time to go home that evening, where we found our house gone, shattered and gone, and we didn't celebrate Christmas at all because we were too busy trying to find our things.

Twenty-nine

Our house—the whole housing compound— seemed to be completely destroyed, blown and blasted, the walls shredded and the roof gone. Christmas was ruined and Mother moved through the wreckage picking up small things—an ashtray, an unbroken cup—and I thought we would never be able to live there again. But huge crews of laughing, sweating, working Filipinos came and it seemed overnight the compound was cleaned and houses were back on their stilts and life had returned to normal—or at least as normal as it had been.

On the ship I had been in a small moving world with the soldiers and Harding, and now in the Philippines it was the same, except that it didn't move and I lived in a house with my mother and father. I saw Father only at night when he came home, and then for less than an hour because he arrived late and I had to be in bed by eight-thirty. Mother I saw little more once she started making the social circuit. Almost never in the day unless she was having the other ladies to our house for cards and then it was too hectic, too pushed.

So my day was spent really with Rom and Maria and I knew nothing of them except for what pertained to me.

This began to change after we had been in the Philippines four or five months.

By then Mother was completely different and I thought once that if I had seen her as she was now but back in Chicago when we were living in the apartment I would not have known her. And I would not have liked her.

Sometimes back then she would come home from work and tell me something that had happened there. She would laugh so hard she would almost pee her pants. And even when I didn't understand the story she was telling, her laughter would make me laugh and soon we would be holding each other and laughing together.

She didn't do that anymore. I had not seen her laugh at all. She would come home and sit in the chair, if she came home at all, and go to sleep—except it was kind of passing out and not sleeping—and Rom would watch her and look sad.

But mostly she didn't come home at all, or very late. She would meet Father after he was finished for the day and they would go to the officers' club and eat and drink and I would not see them until they came in late at night to make sure my mosquito netting was tucked in and I would smell the beer and gin on their breath.

Maria did the housework and cooked lunch or supper when Mother wasn't there, except that she didn't cook anything but rice and sardines. She never left. Even on Sunday, which was her and Rom's day off, Maria stayed. I asked her once why that was, why she didn't go to her family on the weekend, and she shook her head.

"They are gone," she said. "All gone."

I did not know then what she meant but found out later when I heard one of the women talking to Mother that the Japanese had killed her whole family.

So she stayed always at the house and cleaned and cooked and Rom took care of me.

Rom liked to play. He was a man and still he liked to play and I think that's why he started to take care of me. Mother had found some small toy trucks and brought them home once when she was feeling bad about being gone and I played with them in the dirt in the backyard. I had small roads and dirt banks and bridges made of sticks, and I pretended we were fighting Japs and the trucks were tanks, only American tanks, not Jap, and one afternoon Rom came to the back steps and sat watching me for a time.

"They're tanks," I said, making engine noises with my mouth. "I'm attacking over there." I pointed at some dirt. "There are Japs there."

He nodded. "I see. That is good. I will be the Japanese."

And he went to the dirt where I had pointed and made an embankment, and when I came toward him with my toy truck/ tank he made a gun sound and shot at them.

"I have hit you," he said. "You were exposed on that side and I have struck you . . ."

And we played that way the whole afternoon, that first time, and after that we were always together. For a long time we played only in the yard, but one day he showed up with a bicycle. It was one of the Japanese bicycles, olive-drab with fat tires and fenders and a rack on the back for carrying ammunition. He had rigged a small piece of board on the rack.

"For you," he said, "to sit upon."

Suddenly we were mobile. I could not ride a bike yet but Rom could and we went all over the compound, up to the main buildings, past them to the motor pools where they had rows and rows of trucks and jeeps and tanks, and even to the airstrip where there were planes taking off and landing constantly.

My world had exploded, had gone from the yard to as far as I could see and farther. There was just one rule: that I be in when the cannon sounded. But Father was almost never home by then, and Mother only rarely.

The fenced-in area was enormous, or so it seemed to me then. We spent whole days just riding around. It was really a small city and I would sit on the back of the bicycle and Rom would pedal and we would travel. I had learned how to use Mother's small box camera and I took this with me and would take pictures as we traveled.

Some days we would go to the airstrip. We couldn't get right to the edge, where all the planes were kept in long rows, but we could get close enough to watch them taking off and landing and I was thrilled because I had seen them in films—P-51s, C-47s—and now I could watch them "for real," roaring over me or flaring in to land.

There was a post exchange and while they didn't have any candy, ice cream, or treats they did have Coca-Cola. It was the only thing available that I could buy and that I liked, and they sold it in paper cups, warm, with no ice, for ten centavos. The split was two to one so ten centavos was the same as a nickel and while Rom never had any money, not a cent, I could always get a quarter from Mother's purse or from Father when he was drunk and smiley and so we would sit, Rom and I, with the bicycle leaning against the metal side of the PX Quonset building and drink the warm coke and watch the soldiers go by.

Some areas we could not go into and there would be a guard there with a rifle or submachine gun to stop us. They were always nice to me and smiled at me, but the soldiers were not so nice to Rom and looked hard at him and made him show his work paper and sometimes I would have to tell them more than once that Rom was our houseboy and he was doing what I asked before the soldiers' hard eyes would move away from him. One time they made Rom lie down on the ground and put his hands in back of his neck and they kicked him with a toe in the ribs. Not hard, but just enough to make me worry that they were going to hurt him, kill him, just because I asked him to take me somewhere.

The strips right along the fence, on the inside about twenty feet wide, were also forbidden. There were towers with guards and machine guns spaced at intervals, but not all the way, and where the towers didn't cover or where the searchlights couldn't reach they had sentries standing. One night there had been an attack by the guerrillas and we came upon a storage shed that was still burning and I took a picture before the guards could see me. Later Mother developed the film and asked me what the pictures were and I shrugged and said I didn't remember but it wasn't the truth. I did remember. How it looked and how it smelled. But she was drinking then, when she was looking at the pictures, and didn't make me tell more.

"It is as if the war still went on," Rom said one day while we were riding. I had asked why there were so many guards and what they were guarding against. "There are those who do not want it to stop."

"The Huks?"

"That is what the American soldiers call them. They want things to change."

"What things?"

He sighed. We were riding and I held his sides while he pedaled, and I felt the air leave him.

At night, every night we heard the machine guns and once on one of our trips we saw a place by the fence where there was a great splash of blood but no bodies, and when I asked Father about it he didn't answer and neither did Mother and not even Rom.

"All things," he said over his shoulder. "And when all things have been changed they will want all things to change again and when they have changed again they will want all things to change yet again. When I was small it was this way and now it is the same."

"But then it will never end."

"Yes. That is right."

"The war is over," I said. "It ended."

"Yes. But that was different. This is not the same war."

"That makes me sad."

"And me."

There came a day finally when the compound was not enough. We had covered everything. I had played more in the wrecked tanks and we had found a Japanese Zero that had landed and was sitting on the side of a large open area and I had sat in that and pretended to be a prisoner who had escaped and stolen a Zero and was taking it back. The seat was very low and I had trouble seeing over the sides and could not see anything out the front of the windshield at all except for the sky, but the stick was still there and the throttle and I worked them back and forth and spent hours making engine and gun sounds while Rom waited patiently with the bike. And one morning it hit me that we had done it all.

Everything inside the compound was old to me. Rom seemed content to leave it at that and just repeat what we had done, but I had caught him stealing and it gave me power over him and I used it unintentionally at first and then mercilessly.

It was not a big thing, the stealing. I saw him take two cans of sardines from the shelf in the tiny pantry in the back of the kitchen. He put them in the pocket of his pants and turned, and I was standing there.

He said nothing but smiled, a small sheepish smile.

It was on a Saturday and he would be going home to be with his family for Sunday and he would take the sardines home. I knew the houseboys and housegirls stole—the women who came to visit Mother talked about it constantly—but somehow I didn't think Rom would. Maria did, I knew, small things—food, sometimes change—though since she rarely left I don't know what she did with them. But Rom was more than a houseboy, or so I thought. He was a friend. I could not understand a friend stealing from us, though to be sure it didn't matter. When Mother found out that Maria only made sardines and rice she bought cans of sardines by the crate at the commissary and a can or two now and then didn't matter. She certainly wouldn't miss them. But I didn't think Rom would steal and so when I accidentally caught him at it I stared and he mistook my staring in silence for an accusation.

"It is for my family," he said, which I already knew. "I do not take the food for myself but for my family."

The risk he was taking was staggering. I sensed part of it because of the fear in his eyes but did not fully understand how devastating it would be if I turned him in and Mother fired him. He would not work again. In the aftermath of the war there was no help—no aid or assistance of any kind for anybody. His family could starve, he could starve. They could die.

If one seven-year-old boy decided to tell his mother, people could and probably would die. If I opened my mouth, his children could die.

I did not know the depth of this but Rom did, and from that time on—not because I did not tell my mother but because I always *could* tell her—Rom did anything I asked or even suggested that he do, no matter the danger. The threat that I would turn him in was always there from that time on, even when we didn't think about it or even when I no longer remembered it.

And I was sick of the compound. Inside the military area there was much of interest, but after weeks, months, it was more and more of the same. Ride to the PX, drink a coke, watch the soldiers march in the barracks area, visit the airstrip, play in the wrecked tanks and plane . . . always the same.

And outside was a whole new world. We been all around the perimeter road along the fence that circled the compound.

Outside there were places where the jungle—rich, thick, and living green—came almost to the fence, or to the cut-away area that allowed the guards in the towers a field of fire.

In some places there were huts and hovels scattered along the fence, jammed with people, and in other places rice paddies being worked by children—there were few men—and women driving the water buffalo.

Great gray beasts covered with mud to keep the flies off, they had the ability to stick their tongues out and completely up inside their own nostrils and clean the snot out. I watched them through the fence as I watched the jungle and the hovels filled with people—fascinated, drawn to them, but kept apart by the fence and the towers.

I felt not so much protected by the fence as held prisoner, and there came a day when Rom and I went to the bicycle and were heading toward the PX and I tapped him on the back.

"Let's go outside."

At first he pretended to not hear.

"Rom."

"Yes."

"I said let's go outside."

"But we are outside."

"No. I mean outside the wire. Out of the compound."

He was, of course, cornered but he tried to talk me out of it.

"Your mother would not like it."

"She is drinking with the ladies at the club. She'll get home late and drunk and we'll be back by then."

"Your father would not like it."

"He'll meet Mother at the officers' club and come home with her. Come on, let's go outside."

He sighed. "Very well. But it will be best not to tell any person that we have done this."

"I won't. Come on."

He turned the bike and wheeled down the road to the gate and we passed through with a wave—the guards were more concerned with keeping people out than in—and I made the first step in what my mother would, with great horror, call "going native."

Thirty

Actually what we did, going outside the wire without protection, was insane. The Huks were everywhere and white children were at some risk because of their value as hostages. I did not know this and had the added problem of pure white hair. In a land of dark black hair and dark eyes a white-headed boy with blue eyes was impossible to miss, and indeed I was considered such a target that later, when Mother and Father had to spend time in Manila, Ryland was assigned to me as a reluctant bodyguard.

Rom must have known this, but it was his world, the world outside the wire, and he must also have believed that I would be safe because not once in all the times I prowled outside with Rom did I feel the slightest danger. Perhaps it was there and I did not sense it, or perhaps because of my father's job—he was involved in trying to rebuild the Philippines and not involved in the military work against the Huks—I was never threatened, never felt any fear.

That first time we did not do much. I directed Rom to some rice paddies where they were working with water buffalo and we sat and watched them. Boys rode on the backs of the buffalo and they seemed not much older or larger than I was and Rom must have known what I wanted. He motioned to one of the boys who was riding a buffalo and the boy stopped near us. I climbed from the bike.

"Do you have ten centavos?" Rom asked me.

I nodded.

"Give it to the boy and he will let you ride the buffalo."

I nodded again but did not move.

"What is the matter?"

The truth was I was scared. I wanted to ride one more than anything and yet I was scared. But I didn't say that. "I don't know how to drive one of them."

Rom laughed. "Just sit on him. The boy will lead the buffalo. You do not have to drive him."

I ran into the paddy. The boy was shorter than me and probably four or five years older. I handed him the money and he smiled past me to Rom and helped boost me onto the back of the water buffalo. In that instant, in that tiny moment, I changed.

I could never tell Mother this thing. I could never tell her of Rom stealing the two cans of sardines, either, but that was different. That was to protect Rom and maybe a little to let me use Rom, but with the buffalo I could never tell her because she would not let me do it. She would say it was too dangerous, too crazy, too . . . too. But it was something I wanted to do and so I had to keep it secret and that began the new part of my life, the secret part, the nontelling part. There would be many things that I could not tell her, but that was the first, truly the first one.

And it was wonderful. The buffalo had great, curving horns that came back from either side of his head like curving half moons, wrinkled and bony, and his back was scarred and tough but warm and it moved beneath me like a living mountain, plodding as it pulled the one-bladed plow through the mud.

The boy went ahead, pulling a rope that was tied to a ring in the buffalo's nose. At the end of the paddy he turned and swore at the buffalo in Tagalog as he jerked its nose around. The immense beast, towering over the boy so that I seemed to look down on him from a great height, wheeled around and began heading back toward where Rom waited for me.

I rode two more rounds, holding tight with my legs, and when I reached the end Rom lifted me down. I thanked the boy and we rode off down the road on the bicycle.

"If I lived here I would ride them all the time," I said to Rom's back. "I would just ride them and ride them and only come down when it was time to come in."

"But you do live here," Rom said.

"I know. But I mean if I *really* lived here. Like if I was Filipino and not just visiting."

For a long time Rom was silent. When he did speak again, he did not talk of the buffalo or whether or not I really lived in the Philippines.

"How is it," he said, "where you really live?"

"It is a big city," I answered. "Bigger than Manila and not bombed out and everybody isn't poor."

"How is that? Is everybody rich?"

"I think so. I mean everybody works, but they all have food and a place to live and there are lots and lots of cars."

He made a clicking sound in his throat and spat off to the side so that it wouldn't spray back on me. "That is an amazing thing. To have everybody rich. How can that be?"

"I don't know."

"Neither do I."

That first day we did not do much besides ride the water buffalo. Rom was clearly worried about taking me out of the compound and as soon as possible he turned and we made our way back.

The guard at the gate stopped us, but when I told him who my father was and Rom showed his work permit he let us through.

We were home in plenty of time to beat the cannon, which didn't matter because Maria was gone. She'd been loaned to another woman for a day and didn't get home and into bed until just before Mother and Father, and they didn't arrive until I was already in bed and nearly asleep and then they were drunk and fought for a time.

Before they started fighting Mother came into my room and leaned over my bed and kissed me on the forehead. I could smell beer and whiskey on her breath.

"Goodnight, Punkin," she said, but I didn't say anything. I wanted to tell her about going outside the compound and riding the water buffalo but I couldn't so I lay still and she left. I was just about to go to sleep when I heard Maria crying.

She had gone to bed at the same time as me because the woman she'd worked for had been hard on her and made her move furniture, and she'd fallen asleep immediately.

She cried every night in her sleep, but she sounded different this night, louder with more breathing in it, and I thought she might be awake. I wanted to tell her of going outside the compound and riding the buffalo—I had not told her or anybody yet and I was bursting to tell somebody—so I crawled out of the mosquito netting and went to her bed. I lifted her netting and leaned over, close to her ear.

"Maria?" I whispered. "Are you awake?"

She hadn't been, but her eyes opened when I spoke to her. They were large in the light sweeping through the room from the searchlight, large and dark and soft at the corners.

She did not say anything but reached up and took my face in her hands and pulled my face down and kissed me. It wasn't a mother kiss or an aunt kiss but the other kind, right on the mouth, and she stuck her tongue in against my tongue.

I was so startled I couldn't do anything. I had heard enough from the soldiers and sailors on the troopship to know some of the cruder aspects of what she was doing, but I didn't know what it was all supposed to mean or what I was supposed to do. After she kissed me she pulled my head down on her breasts and I was surprised to find them bare. Usually she wore a frayed slip to bed, but she had shrugged it off and she buried my head first between them, small and firm, and then moved it back and forth and twisted it around until her right nipple was against my mouth and then in my mouth.

All this time she was moving. Her hips moved sideways and she pulled me into bed, never taking her breast from my mouth until I was under the sheets with her and then on top of her. She spread her legs until I was between them, and she wrapped them around me and kept moving, moving all the time, her hips thrusting up at me, and I didn't know what to do or if I should cry out or not make a sound. Then, too, there was the other part of it.

Strange things were happening to me. I found that I was enjoying what was happening. The soldiers had talked of this and I knew what a cock and cunt were, sort of, though I was not certain what I was supposed to do with them. My stomach ached intensely, a throbbing, deep ache that started in my hips and groaned up through me, a wondrous joy of an ache that made me move on top of Maria though I really knew nothing of what was happening. I just moved and she moved fast and I sucked her breast and wiggled there on top of her and finally she heaved some more, quicker and quicker, and then she lay still. She did not push my head away, but I could sense that something was different, that it was over, and I looked at her face.

She said nothing but smiled at me and petted my hair and the side of my cheek and I saw that her face was sweaty and the hair at her temples was damp and sticking there and I felt sweat on both of us, sticking us together, and I wondered what to do, what I was supposed to do. The soldiers never talked of what to do afterward. But it didn't matter because in seconds she was asleep. Her eyes closed once, twice, and then didn't open and she was asleep and whimpering, the same small crying, and I rose and went back to my bed and lay awake for a long time thinking.

Thinking of the water buffalo and that I couldn't tell anybody and now this with Maria and how I couldn't tell anybody this either, and I wondered how many other things there would be that I couldn't tell any other person, how many other quick breathing hidden dark and wonderful-awful things that left my stomach aching and my mind heaving that I could not tell another person, and then I slept.

Thirty-one

 There was such waste and wreckage from the war.

Everywhere you looked there was something left from it. Inside the compound it was relatively clean. Prisoner teams from the stockade, watched by guards holding submachine guns, were used to clean the streets, and they picked up any dirt or trash except for the large waste—the trucks and tanks and planes.

But outside the military housing area it was not so clean, and the ground was covered with war trash. It was impossible to find a square foot that did not contain empty cartridge cases or bullets or shrapnel.

I collected them for a time and had a box of brass cartridges, empty and unfired, but there were so many, so many thousands and thousands and still more thousands of them, that I finally gave up.

I tried to imagine how it must have been, and one day while riding outside the wire with Rom I asked him.

"I saw on a newsreel once where a soldier was firing his rifle and each time he fired one of those empty cases came flying out. Is that how they all got here? From soldiers firing?"

He nodded. By this time we had ridden so much on the Japanese bicycle with my hands on his waist that I could feel what he was doing and did not need to watch him.

"I mean for each of these empty cases somebody fired?"

Another nod.

"But there are so many. How could they? They must have fired all the time."

He stopped the bike. We were perhaps a mile from the base but still well out of the city of Manila. Both sides of the road were lined with shacks made of scrap wood and sheet metal and cardboard or bits of blown-apart vehicles. There were people everywhere you looked. Not so many men, but some, and many, many children and women, as thick as the cartridge cases.

"They came up from the city," he said, standing with a leg on each side of the bike and pointing with his left hand while he held the bike with his right. His arm swept.

"They had taken the city and the Japanese were still out here, out at the base, this part of the base, and the soldiers came up from the city, many, many of them. I could not count them all."

"You were here?"

He nodded.

"And you saw them?"

Another nod. "They walked along each side of the road and they shot at anything that moved, whether to the front or out to the sides. They had long lines of men going across the front who also shot at everything. In the center of the road they had two tanks in front like great beetles. I thought they would shoot me. I was hiding in the trees and I stood up and smiled and one of them raised his rifle and I thought he would shoot but he did not."

"You mean they were shooting Filipinos, too?"

"Yes. Some would shoot anything that moved, others would

not. It was a matter of luck or God if you did not get shot. Only that. Luck or God. I was lucky, since I do not believe in God."

Through all this he had been gesturing with his arms to show how the soldiers had come and I looked as he pointed and tried to see it in my mind. All the bullets, all the brass cartridges on the ground. *The noise*, I thought—*it must have been loud.* "Was it very loud, all the shooting?"

Rom nodded. "You could not hear the shots. It was like a great ripping sound, like all the cloth in the world being torn. Machine guns and the weapons of each man and the tanks—all one sound."

He turned and pointed back toward the base. "The Japanese came there, from the base. They set up their lines where those mounds are in the earth and there was a great fight here. The Americans were pushed back once, then again. They lost many men and then some more tanks came and they went over the Japanese. They killed for a long time, the Americans. Teams of men went along the Japanese positions shooting them . . ."

"You mean after they surrendered?"

"They did not surrender. Even those who were not used to fighting, the clerks and cooks, stayed and fought and did not give up and died. Every one of them died. I knew some of them, many of them, and they all died."

"You knew them?"

He looked down at me and smiled. "Of course. They were here for a long time, the Japanese. They needed houseboys and housegirls just as you do. I worked for them."

"But they were Japs."

"Of course. And they were bad. And I am glad they are gone. Still, one has to work, to eat. They lived on the base and they needed servants and they paid—though not as well as Americans pay. I worked for a Japanese officer who lived in the street behind your house."

"Our house! Were there Japs there, too?"

He nodded. "I did not know him, but I saw him several times. The man who lived there. He was a colonel, I think, and he was very fat."

In our house, I thought. There was a Jap there, just walking around, sitting in the chairs, eating, drinking. Using the bathroom. I peed right where a Jap peed. I wondered if Maria knew him. I wondered if he went to Maria's bed and sucked on her breast and bounced on her until she shuddered. "What happened to him?"

"He died. The American soldiers shot him. I did not see the body, but they probably put him in the cave with the others."

"Cave? What cave?"

"Oh, over there." He waved vaguely in the direction of some low hills and ridges beyond the shacks. "There was a cave there with bad spirits in it. Near a small church. Many Japanese soldiers went in there to fight, but the American soldiers brought in the big tractors with blades and covered the front of the cave and smothered them. After they died the Americans opened the cave again and put the bodies of other Japanese in and sealed the entrance again with dirt."

"Can we go to see it?"

Rom shook his head. "Not today. It is too far and we will not get back before the big gun . . ."

"Tomorrow."

"We'll see." He sighed. "There are bad things there. The spirits."

"Tomorrow."

"We'll see," he repeated.

But we did not go the next day or the one after that or as it turned out for many days. Mother and Father were invited to a large party at the house of the new mayor of Manila. There would be many dignitaries there, perhaps even the president of the Philippines.

And their children.

"My child will be expected to be there," Father told Mother. "The boy will come."

Thirty-two

We had been in the Philippines seven months by the time of the party and I had learned many things. Perhaps *learned* is the wrong way to say it. I had come to *know* many things; some of them I did not want to know.

I came to understand in those first seven months that my father and I would never be close. Because of my youth I did not so much think of it that way as sense it. I was seven, almost eight, and we had been apart nearly my entire life. I was not so much his child as a child my mother, his wife, had and he had not known.

He tried. There in the Philippines he tried to make a family, at least with me. He would make attempts to talk with me, ask me what I had been doing or how I liked schooling—a tutor hired by the government came four times a week to teach me—but he was so aloof, so military and dry and rigid, that there was no person there, no living person. He spoke to me more in the form of an interview than a conversation.

"Tell me, boy," he would say. And no matter the question I would answer with a "sir."

"Yes, sir."

"No, sir."

The barrier was too well formed and did not break, partly because of his stiffness, distance, and partly because I couldn't tell him the truth about any part of my life. He would have restricted me forever for leaving the base, would have fired and (I worried) maybe had Rom killed for allowing me to leave, would have whipped Maria and me for what we did in the bedroom at night, and maybe had her killed as well. There was much talk of death and there was machine gun fire along the fence each night and blood sometimes by the wire. I knew Ryland had killed many Japs and maybe others and he would do what my father ordered. It just seemed natural that Father could order Rom and Maria to die.

And so I remained silent, or lied, and we did not become close.

When I was to go to the party it was a special surprise and treat. Or so I thought. But it was a complete dress-up party and I had to wear a small coat and tie that Mother had a Filipina seamstress make for me. When we left for the party—in the jeep with Ryland driving, Mother and me in the back, and Father in the front in his dress uniform—I felt like I was tied up. The tie was too tight, the jacket too binding. I was used to running wild, barefoot with only a pair of shorts on, and suddenly to be strapped in a suit was torture.

But it was still exciting. We rode off the base and by the shacks and into Manila, past the bombed-out area and out into a nicer part, where the homes were large estates. I thought they looked like castles. We finally turned up a driveway and stopped in front of a mansion. There were many vehicles, mostly jeeps and staff cars, parked in the circular driveway in front of the columned house.

Father stepped down from the jeep and helped Mother out. I clambered over the back.

"Stay with the jeep," Father told Ryland. "You will need to watch the boy later."

Ryland nodded, but I didn't understand.

"I thought I was going to be inside with you and Mother," I said, but Father gave me a stern look without answering.

A servant greeted us at the door and led us in.

"Jesus Christ," Mother said. Instead of entering a hallway, the entrance led into a huge open area, an enclosed courtyard open to the sky. It was covered with stretched fine bamboo screens with tiny spaces between the strips of bamboo so that the whole enclosure was lighted with a striped, dappled light that seemed to move.

The courtyard was completely filled with people and food. Somewhere, at the other end of what seemed almost a village, there was music playing. But inside the courtyard there were rows and rows, quadrangles of great clay bowls, three, four feet across, sitting on the floor so that you could walk among them and heaping with food—crab salads, mango salads, shrimp, enormous quantities of rice with different kinds of sauce available.

There were hundreds of people, but even so they could not possibly have eaten all of the food. I wanted to run down the rows, the walkways between the quadrangles, and count how many bowls of food there were but I could not have done it in a week. Or ever. I wanted to tell Rom. He thought of food all the time, and stole food for his family, and I wanted to tell him about all this food. He wouldn't believe it, wouldn't believe that there could be such food anywhere in the Philippines.

But I was not to eat any. I stood next to Father and Mother and we went into a line. I waited and waited and then I was introduced to the mayor of Manila, who smiled down at me and touched my head, the white hair on my head.

And I was done.

Children, it seemed, neither white nor Filipino, were to be

allowed in the main part of the festivities. We were to remain outside and wait for our parents to finish.

Father escorted me to the door and there found Ryland, standing casually by the jeep. He came to attention and saluted when he saw Father.

"Watch him," Father said, returning the salute. "There is some risk of kidnapping. There are many targets here, diplomats and officers."

Ryland nodded and took his submachine gun, oiled and deadly looking, from the rack in the jeep. It was the same one I had carried from the ship. "No problem."

He was to be a combination baby-sitter and bodyguard for the whole evening, and it became clear very quickly that he considered the job beneath him. He had a small glass bottle of whiskey under the driver's seat of the jeep and he took short pulls on it. I sat in the backseat and waited.

And waited.

Ryland ignored me except to give me a dirty look now and then and we sat that way for what seemed like hours. It became dark, Ryland became drunk, other people came to the party, some left, and the boredom was becoming something dead when I heard the sound of children playing.

I had not played with other children since the typhoon. I had seen them, Filipino children, by the dozens, but I was always going past with Rom or they were outside the wire and I was in. I had not seen any white children at all, though I was told there were some on one of the other islands.

The sound of these children, Filipino and loud and clearly having fun, was irresistible. It seemed to be coming from around the side of the building and I stepped down from the jeep.

"Where are you going?" Ryland asked.

"I heard some kids playing."

"They're Flips . . ."

"I don't care. I'm sick of waiting. They'll be at that old party all night and I don't want to sit in the jeep anymore." I started walking.

"Goddamn fucking kid," Ryland muttered, but he brought his bottle and the gun and followed.

There were seven or eight Filipino children around the end of the building. Along the side was a large open space, floored in flagstone with a stone stairway that angled up the side of the building to a balcony.

They had a simple game going. One would run up the steps, then jump off the side back down to the flagstones. Then the next one would run up, go a step higher or as high as he dared, and jump.

The top, at the balcony level, was ten or twelve feet high and I watched them for a moment. One of the children beckoned to me to try it and I started forward, but before I could move Ryland grabbed my coat.

"They're fucking Flips, kid. The only way to play is to be better than they are. Go all the way to the top."

He pushed me, kicking me in the butt for emphasis, and for some reason—the kids seemed to be taunting me to jump and Ryland's voice was rough and frightened me—for some insane reason I did as he said.

Without thinking I ran to the top of the stairway and jumped all the way down.

I kept my legs too stiff and hit with a stunning jar and still, still I would have been all right except that in my nervousness or excitement I jumped with my tongue sticking out.

It was not just the end but well back, over halfway, and my teeth came together with the sound of a cleaver hitting a block.

My tongue was cut virtually in half, hanging by the sinews that run along the bottom, dangling down on my lower lip.

I knew instantly what had happened—the pain was immediate—and I pushed the tongue back in my mouth, clamped my hand over my lips, and ran for the only help I knew.

Mother.

It took less than a minute to run around the building, past the waiting servants, and through the front door. I did not see her at once but ran for another minute or so up and down the alley-ways between the rows of food, jostling people in formal dress, men in light suits and women in beautiful white lace-trimmed linen dresses with high shoulders, and finally I saw her. She was standing with her back to me, talking to an officer in dress uniform, and when I saw her the fear, the pain, all of it came together and I opened my mouth and screamed.

"Mother!"

Except that it didn't come out that way.

It sounded more like a plunger being pulled rapidly out of a toilet. All the time I had been looking for her the blood had been pouring out of the stump, filling my mouth, and when I opened it to scream the blood, under pressure, sprayed in all directions.

Mother didn't hear me, but the screams of women around her as I sprayed their clothing and food with blood made her turn. When she saw me, pouring what must have seemed like gallons of blood out of my mouth and down my clothes, trying to yell and hold my flapping tongue on at the same time, her eyes went wide and she reached for me.

"I've got him," Ryland said. He'd been following me at a dead run, still holding the gun—an armed soldier crashing through the entry to the mayor's house chasing a bleeding child caused even more panic and weapons jumped out of suits on all sides—and he caught me from behind and picked me up. "Come on."

He held me with the same arm that held the gun, expertly used a finger on his other hand to poke the tongue back in my mouth and clapped his hand over it to keep it in, then turned and ran for the door with Mother following. "His father—" she started to yell, but he cut her off.

"No time. Come on."

I began going into shock as we reached the jeep. Ryland

jumped in and started it, holding me in his lap, so fast that Mother barely got in. I saw her slam back into the passenger seat as he accelerated, then I leaned my head on Ryland's chest and thought that it wasn't so bad. Everything seemed dreamy, soft, and I started to go to sleep. I was so tired, so tired, but before I could doze—pass out—I choked on blood and had to open my mouth and let it out again. It flowed in a thick river down between the seats, and Mother looked in horror but said nothing, did nothing, let Ryland do it all.

"He bit his tongue," Ryland said, cutting his words. "Off."

He drove like a machine, the jeep screaming through the night. I saw lights, a blur, felt the roughness of the road, and knew we were going back through the city, back to the base, but the shock still held and I didn't feel any pain.

The ride could have taken minutes or hours or days. It didn't matter. When I started to choke I would reach to Ryland's hand, where it was clamped over my mouth, and he would release me long enough to let the blood drain and then clamp it tight over my lips again and in a time we stopped, suddenly, the tires sliding on gravel.

Ryland hit the ground running, carrying me in his arms, and we went from a darkened world into the bright white glare of the hospital. I had never been in this hospital before but had been past it with Rom on the bicycle. It was a long, low building, made of wood and bamboo thatch with a metal roof. I had seen the large red cross painted on the roof that everybody said the Japs used for a target with their planes when they attacked the Philippines.

Ryland knocked the door open with his shoulder and carried me into the emergency room. There were people coming from all sides, two or three nurses and a doctor. All in white, starched white, crisp white so bright I had to close my eyes.

"He bit his tongue off," Ryland said. "Twenty minutes ago."

"Do you have it?" the doctor asked.

"It's still hanging by a cord, maybe a little skin . . ."

"Hold him."

They flopped me on my back on a metal table. The stainless steel was cold. I could feel the cold through my clothes and on the back of my head. Ryland held me around the chest, jammed me down to the table, and somebody else held my legs.

I was terrified now, scared of the doctor and the pain and what I had done. Mother looked down, she held my hand, her eyes torn with worry the way I had seen her in the hospital in Chicago when I had pneumonia and they didn't think I would live.

"It will be all right, Punkin. Everything will be all right."

But it was different now. I was older and had seen and done more and I knew goddamn well it wasn't going to be all right. They were going to hurt me and I screamed so loud the sound seemed to bounce off the ceiling.

Blood sprayed in all directions, covering all the white and the khaki of Ryland's shirt, those places I hadn't already covered. While I was screaming, the doctor jammed some kind of device in my open mouth, a vise arrangement that held my mouth open. He cranked on something that opened it wider until I thought my jaw was going to rip off.

"Oh, hell," he said. "It's nothing. Just a clean chop." He smiled. "Clean and even."

He reached in with both hands and, without painkiller, sewed the chopped-off half of my tongue back onto the stump.

They could not hold my legs. Every time the needle went into my tongue the pain was so bad that whoever was on my legs lost control and I drummed my heels on the steel table and screamed, or tried to scream. His fingers were jammed into the opening, along with some kind of small hose that sucked the blood and spit out. I tried to bite him, but the vise in my mouth had a spring in it so that it would follow when I opened and then hold. I felt like my jaw was being torn off, and when I looked up there was Mother.

"It's all right," she said. "It's going to be all right . . ."

Eleven stitches. Each one agony. The needle going in, curving, back up through the stump, then pulling, pulling hard while he tied it and snipped it and then again, another stitch, pulling, tugging, jerking, and tying, snipping.

Eleven, and each time it was like biting my tongue off again. Finally, toward the end, I did not cry, did not scream, but lay and hated. Hated Mother for the lie of telling me it would be all right, the doctor for hurting me, Father for bringing me to the Philippines, and most of all Ryland for making me, as I thought, run to the top of the stairs and jump.

When the doctor was finished they took me to a bed in a long room with many beds. Some of them had soldiers in them, but I didn't care. My tongue felt the size of a basketball. It filled my whole mouth and stuck out so far I could see it. And it kept bleeding so that I had to spit in a pan the nurse put by the bed.

"We'll keep him for a day or two," the doctor said. "Just to make sure there's no infection . . ."

"Thank you, doctor," my mother said and I wanted to say, *Why thank the son of a bitch, look what he did to my mouth*, but I couldn't talk, could do nothing but moan and croak.

The doctor smiled down at me and left. The two nurses who had helped him with the operation settled me into bed and propped me up on pillows.

"You have to sit up a bit," one of them said. "Just for tonight, so you won't choke."

And they were gone. All of it, start to finish, hadn't taken thirty or forty minutes—they had been schooled in the war and knew how to work fast and efficiently—but it seemed like years.

I lay on the bed, looking up at Mother who stood smiling down at me, pushing my hair back with her hand and her touch, cool and soothing, did much to calm me, settle me, and I finally began to understand that she hadn't lied and that it would be all right.

Ryland stood across the bed from her, also looking down and also smiling, though his smile didn't look as soft as Mother's. His shirt and the front of his pants were covered with blood.

"That was some jump," he said, and I looked at him and didn't say anything but thought, *All right, you bastard, when I can talk I'm going to tell on you, tell Mother and Father and Father will have you killed*, except that I didn't know if Father cared because he still hadn't come to the hospital.

Then a strange thing happened. Mother hated Ryland, had from that first day. I had heard her talking with Father many times about him and how she disliked him, hated him, wanted Father to get rid of him.

But now she looked up, across me, at Ryland, right into his eyes, and it was part of the same look she used to give Uncle Casey back in Chicago and Harding on the ship. Not the full look but a part of it, a soft edge of it, and I squeezed her hand, tried to make her stop, but the look went on and on for longer than some kisses in movies, the real long ones, and I wished first that it wasn't happening and then that I hadn't seen it.

But I had.

I saw it plain. And then the nurses came and put a needle in my arm, which only hurt a little, with a long tube leading to a bottle. They squirted something else in the bottle and I went to sleep so fast I couldn't even stay mad at Mother and Ryland and the look she was giving him.

Thirty-three

I was in the hospital for only three days and when I went home I had to drink powdered chicken soup mix through a straw at the side of my mouth for two long, dragging weeks. I absorbed a lot of pity in those weeks, from Mother and Maria and Rom, and Mother even backed off on her drinking and being with the women. I did not see Ryland for that time and did not tell on him because I was afraid that he might kill Father before Father could kill him. Instead I moped around, drank chicken soup, and colored in coloring books while I waited for my tongue to return to normal size.

Finally there came a day when they pulled the stitches and it bled only a small amount. The next morning Rom, who had been spoiling me completely, asked if I wanted to go for a ride on the bike.

"I want," I said, "to see the cave." I had not forgotten.

"It might be better not to go there."

"I want to see it."

And so, of course, we went.

The country around the housing compound varied only a

little. Where it could grow, where it wasn't cut back constantly, the jungle moved in. It was so thick it seemed to be a wall.

"You couldn't push a stick in it," I said to Rom while we were riding. "But sometimes I see people walk up to the edge of it and move a little and they're inside. How can they do that?"

"Those are people who were born in the jungle," Rom said. "I was born in the city." There was pride in his voice. "Jungle people can move that way but we cannot. We have changed."

I wanted to be able to move in the jungle that way, to go in there and play Tarzan, but I was too afraid.

"There are snakes as big as my leg in the jungle," Rom said. "They hang in the trees and drop when you walk beneath them. They eat small pigs and children."

I didn't truly believe him and thought he was just telling stories the way Mother sometimes did to scare me so I wouldn't do something. Like when she told me not to use the scissors or I would put my eye out even though I had never seen a person or talked to a person or known about a person who had put his eye out with scissors.

And I would have thought maybe Rom was telling me that kind of story except that one day I had gone into the backyard and the monkey hadn't come at me.

For the first few months each time I went into the backyard and the monkey next door saw me through the cracks in the mesh of the fence he would come for me. These were not light attacks. He was mean, the monkey, stinking and mean, and if I was close enough to the fence he would try to grab me beneath the bottom of the woven mat or through any opening he could find and if he got me he would hurt me. I had been bitten several times— though I hit the little son of a bitch with a board more than once—and when he couldn't bite me or get at me he would sit on the top of the fence and crap in his hand and throw it at me. He didn't do this to any other person and seemed on his best behavior when Mother or Father or Rom or Maria were in the yard except for playing with his pecker. But when I was there alone I had to watch it and spend most of my time in the center of the yard out of range of his arms or his ability to throw turds. One day I went into the yard to play trucks in the dirt and he wasn't there.

I waited. Usually he came screaming, waving his arms, running on his back legs.

There was nothing. Only silence.

When a full minute had passed I went to the fence and peered through the mesh.

At first I couldn't see anything out of the ordinary. Then I saw the wire and the loop that slid on the wire holding his chain. I let my eye follow the chain down and it disappeared into the grass, or what I first took to be grass.

As I watched, the "grass" moved and I saw that what I had been watching was a huge snake. It was almost perfectly camouflaged and blended into the lawn so well that even when I knew what it was I couldn't see it all. The head was four inches across and flat on top and the body was easily as big around as my leg and maybe as big as Rom's leg and the chain that had been holding the monkey disappeared into the snake's mouth.

"Mother!" I screamed and ran into the house. She came out with Maria and Rom right behind her. Rom left and came back with a machete that Father kept in a tool shed on the side of the house.

He climbed over the fence and I watched through an opening as he went to the snake, which hadn't moved yet, and in two chops he cut the head off. Except that it couldn't come all the way off because the chain went down inside the snake to the monkey, which was a large lump about four feet back from the head. When Rom cut the head off the snake thrashed and wiggled some and I saw that it went all the way back to the other fence—it must have been twelve feet long—and I felt bad because I was glad it had eaten the monkey and it wasn't bothering anybody very much.

"He came from the jungle," Rom said. "In the night he came and swallowed the monkey."

And so I knew when he told stories of snakes in the jungle that he wasn't lying just to scare me, but I still wanted to go into the thick green wall and play Tarzan only I didn't dare.

Rom had spoken of the cave and I saw the hill, the back side of the hill not far from the shacks past the gate, and I knew that on the other side of the hill was the entrance to the cave.

"There is a church near there to stop the evil, but it does not always work. It is a bad place."

To get around the hill to the side where the cave entrance lay we had to go through the jungle. There was a packed trail, made by people walking, and so hard the bicycle didn't sink in. But the bicycle wiggled back and forth so much we couldn't ride without falling.

"We walk," Rom said and stopped the bicycle.

It wasn't quiet but it made you think it was almost silent. Something about the jungle made me want to whisper. The light filtered through and made everything seem like we were looking through green Jell-o. The trees and foliage completely covered the trail and there was no direct sunlight, no brightness at all, just the soft green light and the musty warmth and the smell of rotting leaves, and we moved slowly through an impossible din of noise made by birds and insects. The noise was deafening, so continuous and loud that it became nonexistent, like background static on the radio.

I was worried about snakes as big around as Rom's leg dropping out of a tree on me and swallowing me like the snake did with the monkey, and I kept watching the trees overhead and almost missed it when we came out of the jungle.

It was so sudden—like coming through a door or wall—that even Rom stopped.

We had come completely around the hill in the jungle and the trail opened into an almost perfectly circular clearing with bright sunlight and short grass. On the left side of the clearing was a small white church, so white-bright it hurt my eyes to look at it.

On the right side the trail led off into the jungle again, but only for a short distance because the hill rose immediately.

"The cave is there," Rom said, pointing to the right. He crossed himself.

"I thought you didn't believe in God," I said. "But you crossed yourself."

"It is what a man does," he said, "when there is such evil. It means nothing."

"Can we go in the church?" I asked.

"Of course."

"Then we'll do that first and go to the cave second."

He shuddered but I was insistent and at last he nodded. "We will do it that way."

The inside of the church was even whiter, if possible, than the outside and seemed to be freshly cleaned and scrubbed. It was very small and there were four short pews made of hard, red wood and an altar at the end made of the same wood with a little cloth hanging in front of it. There was a cross embroidered on the cloth.

Over the altar, on the back wall, hung a long samurai sword. I knew what it was from pictures in war comic books. They always had a Jap coming at a GI with a samurai sword and the GI would shoot the Jap in the chest or stomach and the Jap would scream.

This sword was longer than I was tall and had a tassel hanging from the handle. There was no case on the blade or anywhere else I could see and the blade shone silver and bright.

"Could I touch it?" I asked Rom.

"I think it would be all right. Do not take it down."

I went to the front and by standing on tiptoe I could just reach the handle and bottom edge of the blade. It was razor sharp, honed so that when I barely moved my finger it cut instantly.

I sucked my finger. "Why is the sword here?"

Rom was kneeling in a pew praying, his knees on the little padded shelf, and I almost asked if praying was also what a man did when he didn't believe in God but was close to evil, but I remained silent. He looked up when I asked.

"I am not sure. There is a story . . ."

"What story?"

He hesitated. "One of the Japanese commanders thought himself a great warrior. It was said that he personally executed many men and that when he did it he used a sword and was so strong that he would take the head off with one blow."

"With this sword?"

Rom nodded. "I have heard that story."

I looked at the blade again and thought I could see stains now, but it might just have been because of what Rom said or the light coming through the small door. "But why would they want to keep the sword here in a church? If it was like you said, wouldn't they want to not keep the sword? If he killed all those people . . ."

"It was said that he loved the sword." Rom stood. "He did not have time to get to the cave. The Americans captured him and when they did they turned him over to the people. There were many who hated him, many he had harmed. They held him down and they used a saw made of the edge of bamboo to saw his head off while they held him. They nailed his head to a post at the entrance to the cave and they put his sword here in the church so that they would always remember him."

He stopped. In the quiet inside the church I could hear water dripping somewhere and the brushing sound of an insect scuttling behind one of the pews. I looked at the sword. It still shone and I thought of the heads it had cut off and what it must have been like to saw the Japanese commander's head off, but it was too far to think, too far away. The inside of the church was so white and clean and fresh and the sword shone so brightly that it all did not seem real—like one of the stories made up to scare me. I believed Rom because he looked scared and soft when he talked about it. I didn't think he would lie to me, but he might just be telling me what he thought was true and it wasn't.

"Could we go to the cave now?" I asked. He turned and looked through the open door of the church in the direction of the cave and crossed himself and his body moved but he clearly didn't want to.

I followed him out. The bike was leaning against the railing of the church steps and he left it there and walked across the clearing to where a faint trail went into the jungle directly toward the face of the hill.

This trail had not been walked very much. The undergrowth had taken it back and even where it had been cut and cleared away it had grown so the grass was waist high and thick and sharp.

Rom led the way, but slowly, looking back twice at the daylight as the canopy closed and we went back into the green world of the thick jungle.

It seemed far to the hill, but we were moving slowly. We came around a small corner and there it was in front of us.

There was a post made of the same red-black wood as the pews, and behind the post there was the cave entrance. Or what had been an entrance. A mound of dirt coated with grass covered and filled what had been the entry, but that didn't hold my eyes nearly so much as the post.

On top of the post, held in place by a large spike down through its middle, was a skull. It was not quite white, a little yellow, the color of mother's ivory bracelet cut into little elephants that Casey had given her, but it was clean with the lower jaw still in place. There were two gold teeth. One on top and one on the bottom.

"The Japanese commander," Rom said before I could ask. "That is him."

I wanted to see it closer. It was ugly but it was one of those ugly things you have to look at and I wanted to get next to it but it was too high.

"Lift me," I said. "So I can see it better."

Rom picked me up and set me on his shoulders and walked closer to the post, closer and closer until my face was right next to the skull.

It grinned at me, the gold teeth flashing, and I thought I could see some parts of him still there, inside the eye holes, that hadn't been cleaned, and I almost threw up except that I looked past the skull and saw a hole in the cave entry. From the better height of Rom's shoulders I could see that it was big enough for me to get through and I knew I had to enter the cave. There would be more in there, more swords and knives and Jap things, souvenirs to take home. Maybe a gun. A real Jap gun.

Rom put me down and before he could stop me I ran to the top of the earth mound and dropped to my hands and knees at the hole.

"No!" he yelled from below. "You must not go in there. There are . . ."

I crawled inside before I could hear what he said next.

With my body blocking the hole it was pitch dark and I could see nothing. The grass disappeared but the earth beneath my hands and knees was firmly packed. I had crawled on the top of the mound for six or eight feet and it started down into the dark when the smell hit me.

It was the smell of the jungle, the almost sweet smell of rotting vegetation or mushrooms and over that, over all, the thick odor of decay.

I moved to the side and found that I could stand and when I moved sideways the light I had been blocking came through the hole and I could see out and down in front of me.

I was in a large room. I couldn't see the back of it and by this time it was all I could do to keep from running out in panic. It seemed endless, fading into darkness, and all about the floor, scattered in all different directions, were bodies.

Or what had been bodies. They had all been reduced to skeletons or near skeletons, some with bits of skin on the face or skull, all in mixed rags of old uniforms and in the light through the opening I saw moving things, large furry moving things, scurrying through the bones and bodies, large fat furry moving things, and I turned to run, trying to scream but my throat caught as the light suddenly ended and something filled the opening.

"Roooooohhhmmmmm!" I screamed in the darkness.

"I am here," he said. He had come through the hole and it had been his body blocking the light. "It is all right. I am here."

"Can't . . . Rom . . . things . . . eating . . . can't breathe . . ."

"They are rats," he said. He held me so I couldn't move. "The body rats. They made the hole. I tried to tell you but you ran too fast."

"Out. Let's get out. Now. Outoutoutout . . ."

He pushed me ahead and we came out of the hole into the light, the green jungle light, and I stood and ran down the hill past the post with the skull on it and out the faint trail to the church where the bicycle leaned against the railing.

I couldn't get enough air. I pulled and pulled and couldn't get enough clean air to make the smell and the thickness and the look of the cave leave my mouth, my thoughts. I leaned over the railing and threw up.

"The . . . things . . . moved . . . ," I said between heaves. Rom had run after me and was holding my forehead while I vomited.

"Rats," he said. "They were body rats. Before the war they just lived wild in the jungle but the Japanese left bodies, many bodies in pits and other secret places, and the rats found them and ate them and now all people call them body rats."

"They were big." I wiped my mouth with the back of my hand, still pulling at the air. "As big as small dogs."

Rom nodded and repeated, "There were many bodies. They ate well."

I started to cry. I didn't want to cry in front of Rom because we were partners. He wasn't a grown-up and I wasn't a kid. We were equals. But I couldn't help it. I had been so frightened by the rats and the cave and now the tears came and we stood that way for a long time—me on the step and Rom standing next to me, not touching me any longer, just standing, waiting for me to finish crying. When I was done he straddled the bicycle and I got on and we rode away, out of the jungle and into the bright heat-light of the afternoon and we never, not once, spoke of the cave again.

Thirty-four

There came a time when Father decided we
should have a vacation.

It was, of course, not that sudden. He looked tired all the
time, his eyes sunken even more than a hangover would cause,
and one day I heard him talking to Mother, or rather listening to
Mother.

"You haven't had a leave in what . . . six, seven years?"

"I know, but there are administrative difficulties just now
and . . ."

"And bullshit! That's all it is. Bullshit. All through the war
with no furlough and now nearly another year and none and
you're going to fall apart. Take two weeks."

"But . . ."

"Take two weeks."

And so Father decided to take one week. We would spend it
up in the Bagiou Mountains in a thatched cabin and just sit and
relax.

And, of course, drink.

But it started right and we packed two valpacks with clothes and put some sacks in the back of the jeep and Father signed out a submachine gun and put it in the jeep as well and the morning we got ready to go Ryland showed up in his own jeep with a bag and his gun. Always his gun.

"What's he doing?" Mother asked. She had just given final, final, *final* instructions to Maria and Rom and was standing by the side of our jeep, ready to get in.

"We are going to the mountains," Father said. "Through some questionable areas. We may need him."

"I doubt it," she said, but her voice was soft.

"He goes," Father said, "or we don't."

Which ended it. We set off on what proved to be an all-day, dusty drive. The road moved away from the city and began winding through smaller and smaller villages, where everybody waved at us and smiled, and I couldn't think that we were in any danger. Once when we had to stop for a small herd of pigs that were in the road several people from the village came toward the jeep and I saw Father's hand move toward the gun in the carrying case. But they were friendly and nothing came of it. I turned to watch Ryland. He didn't get out of his jeep, but he was driving with his windshield down and I saw the barrel of his gun come over the top and lie so that it covered the people coming to the jeep and I thought, *If they do something wrong he will kill them. Not just hurt them, but kill them, and he wouldn't care.*

It made me feel funny—a little scared but in some way strong, too. I was seven and if I screamed or if these people bothered me Ryland would kill them.

We moved on, and in the middle of the afternoon we came around a corner and found ourselves in a mountain village. It was different from the other villages. Much of it was tucked back into the jungle and out of sight, and the people were more aloof. They were still friendly, but they didn't come to the jeep right away when we stopped and there was no begging. There were dogs everywhere. All colors, all shapes, all sizes—village mutts.

Some were loose and many others were tied to trees and posts with sticks holding them by the neck.

"Igorots," Father said, stopping the jeep. Ryland stopped in back of us, but let his jeep come closer than before. The gun muzzle was across the windshield, aimed in the general direction of the men and women in the immediate area. Ryland smoked a cigarette, using his left hand to take it out of his mouth. His right hand never left the gun. I thought that there might be a fight and I would see Ryland in action, but it was not to be. The people were friendly, and Father climbed out of the jeep.

"Why are we stopping?" Mother asked.

"Carvings. They sell wood carvings that are famous. I thought you might like to see what they had."

He didn't have to say it twice. Mother had changed much since coming to the Philippines, and one of the changes was in the business of shopping—what Rom and Maria called going to the market. Rom called Mother "the wolf" because of the way she bargained.

"She will not stop," Rom said to me once. "She keeps at them until they make her price. She is savage."

The Igorots were no fools and were not about to give away anything. One of them, an old man, came out of a hut and put eight or ten wood carvings on a woven mat on the ground and squatted and waited. Mother went to the other side of the mat and squatted. Father frowned and started to say something, then stopped. She pointed to one of the carvings and the old man smiled and said:

"Ten dolla."

Mother shook her head. "Too much."

"Ten dolla."

"Too much. Give three dolla."

The old man spat off to the side and shook his head. "Eight dolla."

Mother spat off to the side. "Four dolla."

The old man watched her spit and his smile widened, his teeth broken and ugly. He was so dark brown he was almost black. "Seven dolla." He held up four fingers on one hand and three on the other with the thumbs folded down.

Mother shook her head and spat again. "Give four dolla."

"Seven dolla."

"Four dolla."

"Six dolla and part dolla."

Mother had him and knew it and wouldn't stop now until he came down to four dollars, or maybe four and a half. But the haggling could go on for a long time and I became bored and started to look at other things.

There were many children around, mostly naked, and mixed in with the dogs were about a million puppies. I'd never seen so many dogs and they all seemed friendly. As I watched, one dog, a white male about a foot and a half high with scraggly hair, went up to a man standing by the doorpost of a thatched hut. The man had been gesturing to the dog, calling him, smiling and making little clucking sounds, and when the dog was close and wagging his tail the man slipped a loop of rope over his neck.

I thought he was going to tie the dog like some of the others were tied, but the loop was attached to a long bamboo tube with all the segments knocked out so it was hollow, and the end of the rope hung out the opposite end of the tube from the noose around the dog's neck. While I watched the man held the tube in one hand, grabbed the rope in the other, and pulled, choking the dog.

The dog fought and tried to get away, then tried to get at the man, but he held it off with the pole and pulled harder and harder on the rope and the dog's eyes bulged and it peed and it died and he wasn't four feet away.

"Mother!"

She had her back to me and was still haggling but turned in time to see the dog die and took me and held me. "What in the hell are they doing?"

Ryland was there. As soon as I yelled he had come from the jeep. No, not come, suddenly appeared, the gun and Ryland, one thing, the barrel of the submachine gun floating left and right like the head of a snake. Father was next to him, though not armed.

The man who had been killing the dog looked at us in puzzlement and Ryland shrugged and sighed, but the barrel of the gun stayed on the Igorots. "They eat them," he said. "They kill and eat them."

"The dogs?" I couldn't believe that people ate dogs. "They eat the dogs?"

Ryland laughed. "Sure. Lots of them do. Flips will eat anything . . ."

While he was talking the man who had killed the dog leaned down, took the noose from the dead dog's neck, and went to a second dog, one tied to a post with a stick holding him and he began to slip the noose over the dog's head.

"Mother . . ."

"I know, Punkin. I know."

The dog was light colored except for a dark spot on his side, a perfectly round spot about four inches across. Like a ball.

"Don't let him kill the dog."

"I know," Mother repeated. She moved to the man with the dog.

"How much?" She pointed at the dog. "How much for the dog?"

The man spoke no English but he knew what Mother wanted and said something in dialect to the older man who had been selling the carvings. The old man nodded and looked to Mother. "He say seven dolla."

She shook her head and spat, narrowly missing the dog killer's bare feet. "Two dolla."

"What are you doing?" Father had come forward and was standing next to her.

"Buying a dog . . . if you will leave me alone."

"What the hell for? He'll just kill another one."

She turned and the corners of her eyes were pinched. "Maybe so. But the son of a bitch won't be killing *that* one, will he? Because *that* one will be with us."

Father opened his mouth, thought better of it, and closed it.

"Two dolla," Mother said, turning back to the owner.

He mumbled something to the older man, who turned to Mother and said, "Six dolla."

She had him and I just waited, held out until she was done and I owned the dog and Mother had spent only two dolla and part of another dolla for it.

I named the dog Snowball because of the round ball on his side and we became inseparable. He was my first dog and seemed glued to my leg.

The rest of that vacation I rode in the back of the jeep with Snowball on a short cord and made Mother and Father allow him in the cottage at night.

The mountains were beautiful. The cottage looked out over the ocean and we were so high we could see down into the crater of another volcanic mountain island some miles away. It was possible to see a lake down inside the crater and villages around the lake.

Ryland was in another cottage nearby, but he was always watching. He did none of the tourist things, didn't care to see sights—which I figured was because he'd seen them already. He'd been with a group in the mountains all through the war, fighting the Japs. Each day when I went outside he was sitting in a rattan chair in front of his cottage with the submachine gun across his lap and some whiskey, which he drank straight from the bottle. It didn't matter what time I came out, he would be there, sitting, drinking in slow sips. I never saw him eat or do anything the whole time we were there, the whole week—just sit. And watch. And if we went somewhere he would follow in his jeep and when we stopped he stopped, but he didn't talk to us, didn't say anything. Just followed and was always there.

One day I took Snowball and walked around the resort area. The cottages were arranged in no pattern, scattered, and there were banana trees mixed among them, growing thick in places so that I came around a corner and saw a larger building. It was the resort headquarters, a lodge of heavy logs and thatched roof and walls and there was an old man, a white man, in a white suit and a white beard. He made me think of Santa Claus except that he was very drunk and sat in a high-backed chair on the veranda of the lodge. He was drinking from a tall glass with a leaf stuck in it at the side so he had to hold the leaf over with his finger when he drank.

"That is a good-looking dog," he said when he saw me. "What kind is it?"

I shrugged. "Just a dog. His name is Snowball."

"What's your name?"

I told him and he nodded. "You must be with that young couple . . ."

I did not think of Mother and Father as being young, but I didn't say anything.

"MacArthur used to stay here," he said suddenly. "Did you know that?"

I shook my head. Snowball was tugging at the rope trying to get back under the lodge, which was up on stilts. Of course I knew who MacArthur was—I'd seen him in *Life* magazine.

"He did. I spoke to him several times when he visited. He was a very brilliant man." He smiled and took a sip of his drink. "A very brilliant asshole."

He stopped talking suddenly and looked over my shoulder and I turned to see Ryland standing there with his gun.

"Hello," the old man said to Ryland.

Ryland nodded.

"Are you with the boy?"

"With his father."

"Ah—for the Huks."

"For anything."

"I see." He nodded and sighed. "You look very capable. A student of the war, I suppose. Could I offer you a drink?"

Ryland shook his head. "I have my own."

"MacArthur used to come here . . ."

I thought he was like an old uncle I had who used to just talk and never say anything so I stopped listening and pulled on Snowball and went back to the cottages.

Later Father told me that the old man had spent the whole war there and the Japanese hadn't bothered him and I thought he must have been a spy or a traitor. The next day I took Snowball and went back, but the old man didn't come out and then we went riding the last day so I never saw him again.

There was a small stable on the back side of the resort and Father rented a pony for me and set me on it. Mother made me wear long pants because she said I would get sore. Of course I had ridden water buffalo, but she didn't know that so I couldn't say that it was sort of the same and I wouldn't get sore and I put the long pants on to ride.

There was a saddle made from a palm-leaf base and a Filipino man who led the horse so it couldn't run away with me, but I made him let go so I could ride alone. The horse had hair that was patchy and coming out in places, but I didn't care. I felt like the Lone Ranger from the radio shows or Gene Autry or Roy Rogers and I decided the horse looked a bit like Gene's horse, Champ, because it was brown and so was Champ.

I rode until I had blisters on my butt like Mother said and still I rode. I rode all day, with Ryland walking along behind, and I pretended I was Gene and looked for outlaws and didn't think about Ryland walking behind. Snowball trotted alongside, only leaving once to put a loose cat up into a banana tree, and nothing else mattered.

But finally it was time to go and the man lifted me off the horse—I fell when my legs hit the ground—and I went into the cottage with my legs two feet apart.

Mother and Father had been drinking all day but keeping it slow and were not too drunk.

"What's the matter with you?" she asked.

"I rode all day."

"All day?"

I nodded. "And my butt hurts."

"Come into the bathroom."

I followed her, Snowball tagging with me, and dropped my pants.

"Oh, Punkin, look at you—you've got blisters."

And she had to prick them and put on something she got from the main office that hurt like fire but I didn't care.

The next day we drove back from our vacation and I had to sit up on one cheek with Snowball next to me in the seat. I winced each time we hit a bump and there were about a million bumps driving down out of the mountains, but still I didn't care.

I was happy then, so happy and we had had a wonderful vacation and almost a family time like I thought all other people had and that's all that counted.

I sat in back cuddling Snowball while Father drove and Mother pointed at things. When we arrived home I told Rom and Maria about the whole trip, all of it, and thought it would last for all time, the good part of what had happened.

Snowball became more than a pet, more than a friend. I brought him inside my mosquito netting at night with me and he would sleep quietly and not mess until the morning when I let him out, and it kept Maria from me for a time. I wasn't sure if that was good because I thought I liked what she did, but I knew it was wrong in some way and Snowball stopped that.

I took to not riding with Rom on the bike, and left to explore with Snowball in the early mornings. I didn't go outside the compound, and wouldn't go without Rom, but I went to all the places we had gone inside the wire only with Snowball for a friend. He sat by the Zero when I played fighter pilot and tried to get inside the tank with me so he could see the holes in the steel and the spots I thought were blood.

I started talking to him. Not like I would talk to a dog but almost like another person.

"I wish Mother and Father weren't like they are," I told him one day while we were walking, "but like some of those others you see in *Life* magazine where they're smiling and happy all the time."

And I think he understood me, or felt how I felt because he stopped and looked at me and seemed to be sad with me. And another time when we were walking along I told him all about Maria's breasts, only I didn't call them breasts but tits, the way the soldiers did, and how I sucked them and how maybe it was wrong and how she moved under me and he listened then, too, only not sad looking. More interested than sad. And in not too long Mother was asking about him.

"Where's Snowball—it's time to eat," she would say, like he was part of the family.

There were different kinds of soldiers on the base. There were American soldiers and they were like Father and the men on the ship and Ryland, except that nobody was really ever like Ryland.

The American soldiers were all friendly and would wave and smile when they walked or drove past.

Then there were the Filipino soldiers. They were a lot different from the other Filipinos. When I went around with Rom, even in the worst parts of Manila or the shacks, everybody was friendly. Sometimes too friendly. They would tickle me, except that they didn't tickle on the ribs but on my nuts and pecker, and they would laugh. I'd be walking and they would reach down and tickle me there and laugh and I would laugh because it would tickle, but it was strange at first until I got used to it.

But then there were the soldiers. They came on the base a lot, for training or to get supplies, and they were dressed just like the American soldiers with khakis all starched and ironed and helmets and guns and sometimes they were put on guard in the compound. They came in trucks, some riding in the back, sitting on each side, holding their rifles with two in the front and they drove fast and didn't wave and didn't seem to be as nice as the other Filipinos. I know Father didn't like them and of course Ryland hated them, but I heard other soldiers say bad things about them in the PX and when I saw them I always got out of the way.

Except one day.

I was walking with Snowball down the side of the road. Rom had to help Maria prepare the house for a bridge party and I was on my own so I had decided to take Snowball to the PX and get a coke. I would drink most of it and pour the rest out on a cupped rock for him to drink, and then I thought we could go to the Zero and play fighter pilot, but a truck came.

There was a long place where you went over a low hill and then the road stretched out ahead and dropped away slightly for close to a mile. There were no buildings on either side, just grassy fields, and on each side of the road was a low ditch with grass almost halfway to my knees. I had walked in the ditch once but I saw a snake there, a small snake with colored stripes, and after that I didn't walk in the ditch anymore but right along the edge of the road.

Snowball walked with me, first on one side and then on the other. It was the middle of the day and hot, with the sun almost straight overhead, and I heard a truck coming from behind.

The dog was right next to me, on the outside, and I turned and stepped off the road a bit to let the truck go by. It was coming hard and things happened very fast, but I could still see it all. The truck was full of Filipino soldiers and there were two in the front seat and the driver was smiling at me, looking at me and smiling. And just as he came near he swerved toward me and it might have been a joke but it didn't matter because when he swerved it put Snowball right under the front wheel.

He screamed as the tire went over him and there was a crunching sound in the scream. He flipped off the side into the grass and I could see his guts coming out his rear end, bulging out, and he kept screaming and the truck kept going, the Filipino troops in the back laughing and pointing at Snowball and me.

It was all so fast. The truck swerved, hit him, and he flopped in the ditch. And then a jeep stopped.

There were four American soldiers in the jeep. They were wearing khakis and helmets and had been following right behind the truck.

One of them had a rifle and he went to the ditch.

"Turn away, kid," he said, only I didn't and he put the rifle to Snowball's head and pulled the trigger. There was a loud crack, so loud it came from inside my head, and the top of Snowball's head blew up and splattered in the grass and he stopped screaming and his legs moved a little more and then stopped, stiff, and then settled.

"We saw it all," the soldier said. He was thin, his face long and thin with dark eyes. "We saw the bastards." The other three men still sat in the jeep and one of them nodded, but the soldier who had shot Snowball wasn't looking at them.

He stood on the side of the road and watched the truck driving away, the rifle hanging in his right hand, and his eyes were sad and I kept looking at him and then at Snowball. He wasn't there. Just his body was there. He was gone and I couldn't believe yet that he wasn't there and the soldier saw me looking at Snowball's body and he said, "Motherfuckers."

Then he raised the rifle and held it hard against his cheek. He was leaning forward, into the rifle and part of the rifle in some way, and he was aiming down the road at the truck, which wasn't so very far yet. The rifle cracked again, once, twice, so loud I jerked, and one of the Filipinos in the back of the truck raised his arm and fell down and I thought the truck would stop but it kept moving.

"Motherfuckers," the soldier said again and he got in the jeep and they drove away in the same direction as the truck, and I was there with Snowball, except that it wasn't Snowball down there in the ditch with his guts out his rear and his head blown off. He was gone, Snowball was gone and the truck was gone and the soldier with the rifle was gone and I could hear birds singing nearby and everything was just the same as it was, except that Snowball was dead, and I walked home and Mother wasn't there so I told Rom about it, and Maria, and I cried a little but Rom said it was just the way of it and when I asked what *it* was he didn't say anything but went ahead with helping Maria clean the living room.

Thirty-five

Sometimes Father's work took him to different places in the islands. One day we went out to Corregidor and I saw the cave where the American soldiers had held out to the last. Father said it was a great thing, what they had done, holding out, but it just looked like more of Manila to me, more of the war; it was blasted and blown apart and there were twisted iron rails and shattered rock and concrete. We went into the cave and saw MacArthur's office, where he had stayed while he was there, and then a hospital room where there had been nurses and Mother cried when a guide told her the nurses had worked with the wounded right until the Japanese soldiers came and took them.

Another time Father had to visit a village on a different island and we went with him in a landing craft, the same kind I had seen in newsreels going into the beaches at Iwo Jima and on D-Day. All across a large bay for two or three hours we went and I ran around in the bottom pretending to be a soldier going onto a beach to fight the Japs and Mother sat in the rear on a small seat next to the driver of the boat and puked over the back. Father

stood at the bow looking over the front ramp that dropped, pretending not to see Mother, just as the driver of the boat pretended
not to see her, except that I saw him look at her when she was
leaned over and her slacks were tight on her bottom, but he looked
away when he saw me looking at him.

I don't know what Father did at the village, but we were there
two nights and three days, sleeping in a small cottage built up on
stilts like our home. Mother and Father only drank a little and
when Father was working Mother stayed with me and it was fun,
just the two of us. She told me stories when I got bored, stories
about when she was a little girl, stories she hadn't told me since
we were back in Chicago, about her mother—she always called
her *Mama*—and we visited some families in the village and ate
with one of them. They had fish and rice and I ate and Mother
pretended to eat and none of them killed dogs or tried to sell us
anything.

On the second day Father came back to the cottage and said
that we were going to go on a canoe trip up to a lake and then
down some rapids.

"Wonderful," Mother said. "I didn't bring anything to wear
in a canoe."

"Dugout," Father said. "They're long canoes and we don't
paddle. We just sit. Don't worry—just wear slacks and it will be
fine."

Early on the third morning we left the cottage and went to a
small river where three long canoes were pulled up on the bank.
They looked like what they were—logs that had been hollowed
out and shaped with axes. Mother and I got in one and Ryland in
another and Father in the third. Each canoe had two paddlers
and there were three boys not much older than I was in addition
to the paddlers and they took some cloth bags of food and we set
off up the river.

The jungle was as thick here as everywhere and grew over the
top of the river and by the time we rounded the first bend we were

in a new world. I pretended to be Tarzan and looked for crocodiles in the water and apes in the trees and that lasted for an hour or more, until the jungle itself became so interesting I couldn't play made-up games any longer.

The canoes were close together and I looked once at Ryland and was surprised to see that he had changed. Normally he was still and strong and dangerous looking, tough, but there was something about him now I had not seen before. The jungle made him nervous and his eyes were never still. His head turned from side to side, flicked almost like a snake or lizard, and every noise—a scream of a bird, the thump of a paddle against the side of the canoe—made his head jerk to the sound. And the gun, the barrel of the gun, went with his eyes—this way, that way, never still. The muzzle went wherever he looked. He seemed almost scared, and Mother saw it and asked him once when the canoes were close, "What's the matter? Don't you like the jungle?"

"No, ma'am," he answered. He was always correct and polite when Father was near. He did not look at Mother while he spoke but kept his eyes on the jungle. "I don't."

"Why not?"

"It kills you."

We kept moving, the canoes sliding against the current, until we came to some rapids. At first they were not fierce. The water shallowed to half a foot and the paddlers jumped out and walked alongside, dragging the canoes for some distance, laughing and talking in Tagalog, and I understood enough to know that they were talking about the wife of one of the paddlers. He was newly married and they were teasing him about leaving her alone.

The rapids grew rougher. It was still shallow, but there were large boulders and the water kicked this way and that and made a great noise. The paddlers motioned us out and we walked on a narrow dirt path around the worst part, while they pulled the canoes upstream with thin ropes tied around their waists. Above the rapids the water calmed somewhat and they beckoned us back into the canoes and I thought we must be like boxes of food to them. Just weight. They talked to each other from canoe to canoe, and laughed and teased, and it was like we were not alive, not there. Out of the canoe, walk, into the canoe—just something they had to carry.

A short way past the rapids the river came around a sharp bend and ended in a beautiful small lake completely surrounded by high cliffs. A waterfall came down what seemed like hundreds of feet across the face of the cliff in a narrow spume that trailed white mist all the way down.

"Oh look, Punkin." Mother pointed. "Isn't it beautiful?"

Even Ryland looked. The water in the lake shone green, like looking through a 7-Up bottle, and the green light went up into the falls somehow and made them sparkle.

Where the river rushed out of the lake the Filipinos had fashioned a bamboo mesh net, to keep anything from shooting off downstream, and above this mesh the lake was still and soft-looking and there was a curved beach that sloped into the water.

They pulled the canoes ashore below the mesh dam and we walked up the short path to the beach area. The paddlers had brought blankets and from the sacks they took dark bottles of beer, which they put in the water to cool, and they spread the blankets and took food from the bags. There were large wooden bowls and rice and chicken that tasted spicy and some meat that I didn't eat—I suspected all meat to come from dogs—and a fish sauce for the rice that the Filipinos ate but we didn't.

They spread a blanket apart from us and we sat on our blanket to eat, except for Ryland, who took a beer and sat off to the side with his gun. Mother handed food out and as soon as I'd taken a bite I put my bowl down.

"Can I go in the water?" The beach was clean and unmarked and sloped gently into the water and seemed made for wading.

"You can't swim, Punkin."

"But it's shallow, and I won't go in over my knees. I promise."

She looked at Father but he was leaning back with his eyes closed, a beer propped on his stomach, and she slowly nodded. "I guess it will be all right. But stay in close where I can see you . . ."

I was gone before she could finish. The water was deliciously cool and clear and I waded and made sand dams and houses along the edge and would have been content except that I saw the log.

It was long and waterlogged enough to be half submerged. A perfect crocodile. I became Tarzan at once and stalked it with a wooden knife and attacked it and it rolled and rolled on me the way Tarzan fought a crocodile in a movie I had seen with Mother and Uncle Casey.

I straddled it and continued the attack and when I finally had killed it the log had drifted and rolled far enough from shore that I could only just touch bottom with my toes. Mother was lying on her side talking to Father, who seemed to be asleep, and I climbed onto the log and tried to paddle it back to shore without her seeing how far out I had gone for fear that she would order me out of the water.

But the log was heavy and was out far enough now to be caught in the current of the river moving through the lake and out the mesh dam. No matter how hard I paddled it seemed to move the other way, away from shore and into the main channel of the river. I was into depth now, over my head—even stretching from my straddled position I couldn't feel the bottom—and I was a little afraid.

I still thought I had control. The log was holding me up, just, and I saw that we were moving closer to the dam and I thought I could grab the mesh of the dam when we moved close enough and hand-crawl my way back to the side and shore.

But the mesh was weak and tattered beneath the water and the log, soaked with water, heavy and massive, was like a tank. It hit the mesh and without perceptibly slowing tore through and headed downstream to the rapids with me aboard. I made one feeble grab for the broken dam, but it was torn away by the current and I was gone.

Caught in the rolling water the log began to rotate and dropped me off sideways. My feet found the top of a boulder and hung for part of a second so that I was standing with my head out of water with the current taking me downstream.

Everything had amazing clarity. Mother still had her back to me, lying on her side talking to Father, and he was half dozing. Ryland was looking up at the edge of the cliffs around the lake, where the jungle showed. The Filipinos were sitting on their blanket chatting. Nobody was looking at me.

And I was going to die.

All that in half a second. The current would tear me off the rock and I could not swim and I would die and nobody was watching, nobody could see, and I opened my mouth and screamed.

"*Mother!*"

And another half a second. All so clear.

She turned over, saw me, her eyes wide in fright. Father starting to sit up. Ryland's head coming around, the muzzle of the gun dropping as if to some new threat.

And a boy. One of the Filipino boys in shorts and a tattered shirt leaping forward, heading for the bank in a great bound.

Then nothing but water. The current had me and I went down, trying to scream for Mother again. I went into the water and the bubbles swirled up and around me in some light, some strange light. I could not tell which way was up and could not have done anything about it if I could. I tumbled, water rushing into my nose and mouth, and I wanted to scream, scream my life away, scream in the mad panic that took me, but the water took that, took everything away.

Then hands.

I fought them, grabbed and fought at them, but they were strong and they grabbed my hair and in an explosion, in a burst of frothing bubbles and light, I came into the air, the sky, saw it all and then felt rocks and sand as he dragged me up onto the shore.

As soon as I felt the bottom I lunged, trying to leave the water. I hated the water. Hated all of water. The boy was in my way now and I slammed up onto the bank and kept fighting, clawing and pulling myself, until I was jammed against Mother's legs, heaving, crying, choking, and puking.

She lowered to her knees and held me, squeezed me and kissed me all over my face. "Oh, Punkin, I thought we'd lost you that time. I was so sure and he saved you . . ."

She looked past me and I turned to see the boy standing there.

He was not bigger than me, standing. And thin, very thin. One of the paddlers was his father and he came over to the boy and patted him on the head. Father still sat on the blanket. He had snapped upright while it was all happening but was frozen now, as was Ryland.

"I wish to give the boy money," Mother said, very properly, to the father who spoke English. The boy did not. "I wish to pay him for what he did."

The man shook his head. "We do not want pay."

Mother took a breath. "No. Not you. I wish to give the boy some money. Tell him. Please."

The man spoke to the boy in Tagalog and pointed at Mother. The boy smiled and shook his head. "No."

"Please," Mother said. "Tell him please. I want to give him something."

The boy shook his head again and this time looked directly at Mother's face and spoke rapidly. I didn't understand much of what he said, but the father translated. The father's voice was very correct and sounded very proud.

"He said thank you, but he will not accept payment for saving another's life. He says it would not be correct."

Mother looked at the boy for a long time, then nodded. "I see.

Would you tell him then that I thank him. That a mother thanks him for saving her son's life?"

The father told that to the boy and he smiled at Mother.

"And would you ask him if it would be all right for me to hug him," Mother said.

He spoke to the boy again and the boy's smile widened and he nodded shyly. Mother went to him and picked him up and hugged him, picked him right off the ground and held him and hugged him until I thought his eyes were going to bulge. Then she set him down and came to me and took my hand and started walking toward the lake.

"What are you doing?" Father had been sitting, watching all this with a small smile, and he stood now.

"He has to go back in the water," Mother said. "Right now. If he doesn't he'll never go into it again. He'll be afraid of the water the rest of his life."

She was right. I was terrified. I dug my heels in and fought her, but her grip was like steel. She marched across the sand, dragging me. I left two furrows in the beach where my heels dug and she pulled me into the water—by this time I was screaming and clawing at her with my free hand—until it was up to my waist.

"There, there, Punkin, it will be all right. It will always be all right." She kneeled in the water in her slacks and held me until I was still, shivering, looking down at the green water all around.

"See?" she said. "It's not so bad, is it?"

"I hate it."

"Think back now." She held me tight and kissed my forehead. "Just a few minutes ago you were having so much fun. Think back to that and wade along the edge and play in the sand like you were. Just think back to when it was fun and you weren't afraid and you liked the water . . ."

She made it almost a song, the way she used to sing to put me to sleep and the way my grandmother sang Norwegian songs, and the sound of her voice took the fear away, or almost all of it away, and in a few moments she was sitting with me in the water at the edge of the lake playing in the sand and I wasn't afraid at all. We made some castles and dams and roads and I would pretend to be a bulldozer and scoop water and sand up to make things, and after a time I looked around and she was gone, sitting with Father on the blanket watching me, and I was playing and it didn't matter that I was in the water, except that I didn't go close to the dam or over my knees and couldn't look into the deep green part of the lake for a long time.

Thirty-six

 It all blew apart on Christmas in the year of
1948. Much had happened in the meantime.

We had been in the Philippine Islands for just two years.

I had become by this time almost completely Filipino. I could
speak the language roughly, could swear in it with some smooth-
ness, could gesture in it obscenely with great filth and was starting to think as a correct Filipino—which is to say I disliked all
white soldiers, most white people in general, and thought of them
as enormously rich, powerful, inferior assholes.

Rom and I lived on the streets as soon as we left on the bicycle
each day. Sometimes we would go to his place and he would visit
with his wife and children. They lived in a shack made of boards
and cardboard with pieces of metal. His wife's name was Imelda
and she was short and should have been fat but was thin with a
round face. They had two rooms in the shelter and I would sit in
the corner, squatting on my heels in the dust as the Filipinos often
sat, and watch while she cooked rice we had brought and opened
sardines and fed the children. There seemed to be dozens of them
and they ate like puppies, grabbing with their hands and jamming

the rice into their mouths—like Maria ate rice only messier—and I always smiled when they ate, and I felt good about being in Rom's house even though it wasn't a house.

Often Rom and I would take things we had stolen—food from our pantry, cigarettes that I had taken from Mother's purse or from the purses of other women who came to visit her—and sell them on the black market for money that we would split evenly. Rom gave his money to his wife and I spent mine on Coca-Cola and a sweet sugarcane confection sold in sticky cylinders.

I had even learned to love baloots. They were a food that made Mother ill thinking of them—a baby duck killed inside the egg just before it hatched and then allowed to sit in hot sand and rot inside until it became almost a liquid-jelly combination. The first time I cracked a shell—they cost ten centavos—and tried to eat one as Rom did, slurping it all out at once, I nearly vomited.

But he ate them with such relish that I kept trying and soon I could crack the end off the shell and let the contents slide down my throat with ease. They were especially good chased with warm Coca-Cola.

The upshot of my going native—along with my almost nightly visits with Maria—was that I no longer knew my mother or father. Truthfully I didn't see them very much and in some ways did not *want* to see them. Father was a stranger, and Mother, through drink and the changes brought on by being with the other officers' wives, was fast becoming somebody I no longer knew. They were drunk almost all the time now. Father would abstain while he worked, while he was gone for the day, but every night they drank and every night that they were home and drinking they fought. Rom would hide on his sleeping porch and I would get in my room with Maria and they would go at each other until one or the other would pass out.

I hated it all, all the drinking, and I hated them.

Christmas 1948.

We had done Christmas the year before but the big storm had

come in and ruined it, torn everything apart, and so there hadn't been a real Christmas like we used to have back in Chicago.

"This year we're going to have a real Christmas," Mother said in my room one day. "We're going to do it right and be a family." Her voice was soft, but her eyes had that hard edge they got when she became angry. "There's been too much of this other business, hasn't there? Too much of running around and playing cards . . ."

And drinking, I thought, but I didn't say anything. I was so happy then, that she was with me and we were going to have a real Christmas again, that I didn't want to say anything to spoil it.

And she tried. As Christmas came she tried. She cooked good things and I helped, the way I had done back in Chicago and visiting Uncle George and Aunt Margaret up at the store on Rainy Lake in Minnesota. She made *lefse* and cooked canned hams and some canned turkey and made bread and the house changed. The smells changed from jungle smells and she tried to make it not be the Philippines.

She found a tree somewhere, a real Christmas tree with real needles, and we made decorations for it out of colored paper. I made an angel for the top with cotton pulled out long for hair and Mother used the spirals of metal from the tops of coffee cans to make hanging icicles and I think it would have worked, I think things would have gone back to normal.

Except that I rode with Rom and was not there all the time and because I wasn't there I think Mother went back to the way she was, to drinking and going to parties.

Then the other thing happened, the thing that made it all so that it could never go back again.

Rom and Maria were both gone and Father had to work late and he sent Ryland home for something, to get something. I don't know. I was in my room playing and Mother had been playing bridge and drinking all afternoon with the bridge ladies and I heard the jeep pull up but thought it was Father and so didn't come out because they would just be drunk and fight.

But it wasn't.

In a little while I heard voices and knew it was Ryland, and then I heard Mother say, "Oh . . ."

Just that way, that soft way, and I came out of my room. I wasn't tiptoeing but walking quiet, a little quiet, and I came in and saw them in the kitchen.

Mother had her back to the kitchen counter with her butt kind of up on it and her dress jammed up and Ryland was against her, up against her, and was reaching for his belt to drop his pants and I stood and watched them for part of a minute, standing Filipino-like on one leg with my right foot raised and resting against my left knee and then I said, "Does this mean I have to call him Uncle?"

Mother pushed Ryland away and pulled her dress down and he hooked his belt back and buttoned his pants and Mother came over to me and slapped me once across the face, so hard my ears rang and I worried that my tongue would come loose.

"Go to your room," she said. "Now."

But I didn't. I stood for a long time, my face smarting where she'd hit me, and then I raised my hand and slowly slid the fingers on either side of the middle one down, peeled them back the way I had learned from the Filipinos, and I looked at Ryland and gave him the finger and said, "Fuck you."

Mother hit me again, harder, and I turned and went to my room but I didn't cry. Not then and I thought not ever. I thought I would tell Father about it, about Ryland, and he would have Ryland killed and maybe Mother. But I didn't.

I didn't because it was Christmas Eve and Ryland left and Mother came in and cried, sitting on my bed, the netting hanging down in back of her, just sat and cried.

"I don't know, Punkin, about all this. I just don't know anything anymore."

"You hit me. Hard."

"I know I did and I'm sorry."

"You were fucking Ryland."

She flashed again, her eyes almost burning, but did not hit me. "Don't say that—not that way."

"But you were."

"I can't stand this," she said. "I can't stand it anymore. All of this . . . It's crazy. It's all crazy now."

She drank the rest of the afternoon alone, drank beer and then whiskey, pouring the whiskey into a glass and sipping it, and then Father came home and it was as if none of it had happened.

"We have to make a big meal," Mother said. She was in the kitchen, leaning against the same counter as when Ryland was there, and I thought of telling Father, but it was Christmas Eve then and it didn't seem right and she looked so happy, weaving and smiling at Father and me, that I didn't.

I thought that somehow it would work out. She was terribly drunk, but I thought it would work. Maria and Rom were both gone for the two days of Christmas—Rom to his home and Maria to work at an officers' club celebration. Mother started to put plates on the table and only dropped one. Father was drunk too, though not as much, but there was a happy feeling, a good feeling, and Mother laughed in the old way so that it made me want to laugh.

The dinner was strange. She put some canned ham on a plate and put it in the oven and then some canned potato salad she had prepared and we each had a fork and we ate cold canned ham because she forgot to turn the oven on and cold potato salad, but it tasted good even if I was the only one to eat.

They kept drinking.

And after I had eaten Mother said, "Now we have to decorate the tree."

Which I thought was crazy because the tree had been up for a week and was already decorated. But we went into the living room and Mother took some of the balls and ornaments off the tree and handed them to me and to Father and said, "Decorate the tree. It's traditional." Except the words were all blurred, mushed together. "Have to do it on Christmas Eve."

"But Mother . . ."

"Do it!" She weaved. "Have to do it . . ."

I put the ornament I held on the tree and Father did the same—he weaved so badly that he almost fell in the tree—and then Mother went to the screen and looked outside.

"Should be white," she said. "Should be all white with snow . . ."

Father stood in the middle of the living room, holding a drink—straight whiskey in a glass—and looked at her, swaying back and forth. He said nothing.

She turned to him. Her eyes, drunk as she was, took half a second to find him, hold him. Then they tightened.

"You hear me? It should be white. There should be snow."

I thought Father shrugged, but I was standing by the tree and it was hard to tell from off to the side.

"It's the tropics," he said. "It doesn't snow. It's different here."

"Goddamn it, there has to be snow!"

"I can't help it."

"No snow." Mother's voice hissed. "No fucking snow."

"But it's tropical," Father repeated. "It's not the same . . ."

She went crazy. She threw her drink at him and started to walk in circles. "No snow—all bad. No snow."

She rubbed her face and pulled at her blouse and looked out the screens again and then back to the tree. "Snow."

She went into the kitchen and swung around, looking. "Snow."

Then into the hallway, the bedroom, and the bathroom. There was a large sack of cotton balls in there we'd gotten from the hospital when my tongue was still bleeding and she grabbed it, made her way back in the living room, bouncing off walls, falling once.

"Snow."

I still stood by the door, but Father had put his drink down and tried to stop her.

"Snow . . ."

She grabbed balls of cotton from the sack and threw them up and on the tree, but they wouldn't stick. When they fell she snatched them from the floor and threw them back up and when they still didn't stay she tore them apart and threw pieces of cotton up and onto the tree, tore each ball in pieces and threw the pieces high and let them fall, handfuls of them, wads of them, kept throwing them up and watched them fall until the tree was white and they were in her hair and it was white and all the time, all the time, Father stood with his hands half raised, watching her, and I thought I had never seen her this drunk.

"Snow," she said, over and over, in a quiet little hissing sound. "Snow, snow, snow . . ."

But it wasn't just drinking. Not this time.

She didn't stop and she didn't drink any more. She kept throwing the cotton up until it seemed that it really *was* snow, falling and falling in a white cloud, until Father finally took her by the arm and led her into the bedroom and put her to bed and then took a kitchen chair into the bedroom and sat next to her, next to the bed all night.

I went to bed but I didn't sleep until almost daylight. When I awakened it was halfway through morning and Father was in the kitchen cooking some bits of ham in a frying pan.

Mother was sitting in the living room on the couch. There was cotton everywhere and she looked awful, her eyes red and her hair tousled. I sat in the chair across from her. She was holding a cup of coffee and when she took a sip her hands shook.

"Merry Christmas," I said, and I meant it, because it was Christmas and the night was over and we should open the presents, but it made Mother's eyes tear up and she set the cup down and held out her arms.

"Come here, Punkin," she said, and I went to her and she hugged me.

"I have something to tell you," she said. "We're going home."

"But this is our home . . ."

"No. It isn't."

"Is home where there is snow?" I asked, thinking of the night before and how she had been and she nodded.

"Yes."

And I thought that she didn't mean it and that we couldn't go because there was Father and he was still a soldier and there was Rom and Maria and baloots and watching the airplanes or playing in the wrecked tanks or seeing the water buffalo in the paddies and Manila and Rom's family and the laughs of the people on the street and how they tickled me and Snowball and the mountains and the cave and the typhoons and all of our life now, all of our life was here and we couldn't leave, but I was wrong.

I was wrong.

We left in just six days.

Epilogue

The plane was huge, seemed bigger than the ship we had come on—a Pan Am Clipper with two floors and a spiral staircase. I was scared at first because I remembered the plane we had picked up on the way over and the sharks, but when it took off and started cruising—except for fuel stops we flew almost constantly for three days—the fear left and I ran around making life impossible for the stewardesses.

They pulled beds down at night just like on the railroads and we slept the first night and I was still excited and awakened every time the plane bumped.

We had left so fast that I still felt like we hadn't gone. Rom cried when Mother told him and Maria kissed me and held me and cried and then they took their small bundles and left and I wondered who they would get to work for next, but I still didn't believe we would leave.

But Father made the arrangements and drove us to the airstrip where a military plane took us on a short flight to another island where the seaplane picked us up and all in a rush, all in a whirl, without stopping we were on our way back.

After the first day of flying and all the pop and candy and food I could eat, after the initial excitement was gone, I sat in the seat next to Mother and stared down at the water, endless miles of water with small white spots on it from the whitecaps, and tried to remember all the things from the Philippines. All the little and big things.

"I want to go back some day," I said to Mother.

She nodded. "If you like. When you get old enough."

"Will you go with me?"

"No. That's over now, all finished."

And of course I believed her. Believed that all things would be different now because we were gone from it, gone from something that had been good at first and then maybe not so good.

But it wasn't. Not everything changed and not everything remained the same. We flew back across the Pacific, back into our lives where Father would follow and retire from the army and I would grow and marry and remarry and remarry and join the army and drink into drunkenness and stop drinking and learn to love my father more than I thought I ever could and try to learn to write and they would die, Mother and Father, and I would have children and *they* would have children and none of it was over, not finished.

And it never would be.

Other books by Gary Paulsen
available from Harcourt Brace & Company
in Harvest paperback editions

Clabbered Dirt, Sweet Grass

The Madonna Stories

Winterdance

Printed in the United States
141978LV00004B/61/A

9 780156 002035

Made in the USA
Monee, IL
13 July 2021